Road Tales: A Raw Education

By George Wedel

ROAD TALES: A RAW EDUCATION. Copyright ® 2011 George Wedel

All rights reserved. Printed in the United States of America. No part of this book may be used or reproduced in any manner whatsoever without written permission except in the case of brief quotations embodied in critical articles or reviews. For information address Wedel Enterprises, 1520 Thrush Terrace, St Louis, Mo. 63144
roadtales@charter.net

ISBN-0615445047
ISBN- 978-0-615-44504-5

10 9 8 7 6 5 4 3 2 1

Acknowledgements:

People have asked me if I believe there is a God. I answer, NO, I don't 'believe' there is a God----I KNOW there is a God. He's the only one that could have gotten me out of the messes I've gotten myself into. Thank You.

I would be remiss if I didn't mention a few people instrumental in this endeavor. First and foremost, my wife, Mary. Without her wisdom, grace and tolerance I would perhaps be in jail or dead---or both. Mike Rosenthal of 90 Degrees West, whose timeless patience at formulating these pages into book form has brought the dream to reality. And John Juelfs, childhood friend and artist extraordinaire who designed the cover. And to the many others who encouraged me to put my stories to pen.

"Don't tell me how old you are, or how much education you have; tell me how far you have traveled----then I will know."
       Anonymous

Table of Contents

1. Great Halls of Education
2. Up, Up and Away
3. Pick a Number
4. Up Against the Wall
5. The Last Christmas
6. A Connecticut Yankee
7. 1st Day in the Old World
8. All That Glitters
9. The Key
10. The Boat to Ibitha
11. Back In Barcelona
12. Further South
13. The Port and a Ship South
14. The Canaries
15. Northbound
16. St. Louis Flashback
17. Deutschland
18. The Pop Festival
19. The SS Officer
20. Hamburgers
21. The University
22. The Way to Amsterdam
23. Cheap Sleeps
24. The Best of Cities
25. The Big Idea
26. Heading Out
27. Tito's Yugoslavia
28. Toes
29. May Day
30. Cradle of Western Civilization
31. No Man's Land
32. Back in the West
33. Blood Money
34. Voices from on High
35. Delphi
36. Athens
37. A Way Back North
38. The Coastal Road
39. Summertime in Paris
40. The Riot
41. English and England
42. You Yanks
43. The Southern Coast
44. George V
45. Back in Amsterdam
46. Because I Like to Get High
47. Father Knew Best
48. H H
49. Love on the Lake
50. Thumbs Out for Scandinavia
51. Copenhagen
52. The Danes
53. Two Is Better Than One
54. The Ferry
55. The Cavalry Arrives; No It's the Navy
56. Homesick
57. Heading Home

1. Great Halls of Education

The main hall was on a bluff overlooking the fertile Missouri River bottoms which stretched for miles before they sank beneath the muddy waters of the Missouri. It was a late 19th century structure made of limestone with long leaded windows and a tall tower at one end. The building itself portrayed power, authority, and longevity as if it were Boaz and Jachin holding up King Solomon's Temple. The school was on the side of a steep hill that descended into the sleepy, laid-back town of Parkville just north of Kansas City Missouri.

It was here, at Park College, that I hoped to achieve some higher calling---not yet heard---in these halls of higher education. But it was not to be. I didn't hear the calling and I only made it through the first semester.

Park was a four year liberal arts school that my mother attended before going to nursing school. I had applied to two colleges. One of which found me unsuitable. My mother later told me she doubted very much if I would be accepted to Park. But I was. Seems enrollment was down and they'd let just about anybody in.

The buildings had character and class—the students I met didn't. It appeared to be a haven for rejects from the east coast, mainly New York and New Jersey. In fact, by the accents you heard all over campus you'd of thought you were back east.

There were only about half a dozen of us from the Midwest and they seemed to think that if we hung around together we'd appear cliquish or exclusive. But it didn't bother the east coasties to band together and exclude us.

We locals were referred to as hicks--- hayseeds or hoosiers. This is where I felt my first real sense of prejudice—that narrow, intolerant bigotry—and it was directed at me! I guess you might say it was a part of my 'higher education'. Now I must say, if that would have happened in high school, there would have been a knock down and drag out 'discussion' and it wouldn't have happened again, at least not to my face. But that was impossible here—there were too many of them. And I vowed before I came here I wasn't going to get kicked out of school.

~~~~

"Snorkey"—what's that for a name?—was a guy from "Lon-GiLand" who would be my roommate for the semester. He had brown hair, brown eyes and was about 5'10 with a round face on a weak frame. We stayed in the oldest dorm on campus, which meant no AC, too much or too little heat, and antiquated facilities; none of which bothered me. Heck, I was just glad to be away from home and on a new adventure. Course, the east coasties said it was because I was a hoosier!!

Everybody was in that getting acquainted mode. Lots of big Bull sessions, all seemingly friendly but in reality there was a lot of weighing and sizing each other up to see who was cool and who was not. After one of these, I knew Snorkey had more wildlife, trees, and fauna in his back yard on Long Island than I ever did in St. Louis.

After a few more of these story telling contests, when most of us were stoned and letting go, it became real clear that I had done more dope and been further a field than any of them. Even the "greatest" in the dorm---the seniors who looked the part of the "real cool hippie type" with long black curly hair down to their shoulders and little dark shades in wire rimmed frames and driving little sports cars were as phony as the day is long.

It's where you've been and what you've done, not what you wear or what you drive. That you can buy!

~~~~

A year earlier in 1968, a friend of mine and I hitch hiked out route 66 to California in the summer of our junior year in high school. We got stuck in Needles and Barstow and it was hot as hell in the desert. We slept in missions and under piers and rode freight trains back through the desert and across the Colorado River. And we met a lot of interesting people---real people, not so my fellow students from New York. They did have one common trait that was predominant through out the entire school population. That was 'liberalism'. And like a little sponge or slowly developing cancer, I was soaking it up and leaning left and ever lefter.

Usually, there were political discussions after dinner in the cafeteria. But since I was an ignorant hayseed from Missouri, I wasn't allowed to participate in any meaningful way. And to some degree rightly so---since I was more interested in hunting and fishing and the girl sitting next to me in class, than the class warfare of Karl Marx and Frederick Engels. Now their theories sounded pretty good at the time. Remember I was growing my left wing roots. Those theories didn't work mind you---but I don't think Karl did either. Didn't he just hang around the library of

London thinking this stuff up? We did have one thing in common, which to me, was a shocking revelation. We were all members of the BOURGEOISE!!! And to think—at the age of eighteen I didn't know that.

~~~

The Vietnam War was in full swing in 69. Walter Cronkite told us about it everyday on the CBS evening news. Such high body counts—we had to be winning, didn't we?

The draft had become a lottery---to make things fairer of course. The first draw was December 1st, 1969. That was my lucky year!!!! My number was 347. Trouble was, that draw didn't apply to me. Mine was the next year, in July, and I think the bastards just subtracted because my number ended up being 16. But that's next year, I'm getting ahead of myself.

The elitist's from back east were obviously worried. The night of the drawing was intense and dramatic. Each reach into the hat held the future of literally thousands of young men. Whether they could continue their education or be forced to go and fight a war in the jungles of Vietnam.

Vietnam, where the hell is that anyway? Some of my friends joined up. My oldest Brother was there right now, on an aircraft carrier off the coast, loading bombs onto the wings of aircraft that flew missions for up 20 hours.

Since my number was going to be drawn next year, for me it was a lesson in observation. Before the draw there was such big talk in the dining room about what this guy or that guy would do if their number was picked. And it came clear to me that most of these "best and brightest" from back east were here for their II S. That's not a degree, that's a deferment. If you stayed in school and took at least 12 credit hours per semester you'd never see a jungle---except at the zoo. But oh, such big brave talk.

I heard about a bunch of draft dodgers that went to an island off the coast of Newfoundland and fished for a living. Now that struck a chord, seeing how I liked to fish.

Ya know---I met one of those guys from New Foundland, in a rural area in the province of Quebec. We were both "back to the landers" so to speak. He rented a farm house with a nice garden plot; I cut a bunch of trees down and built a log cabin on a lake, with no electricity or running water. He couldn't make it—I left eleven years later with a wife and two kids under my arms.

~~~

There was talk of a big demonstration being planned at a school up in Ohio called Kent State. A few of us got together and decided to go. It was all planned out. The day we were leaving, the car belonging to the guy who was supposed to drive, broke down. No plan B, so we stayed home. "Divine Intervention"!??

Those of us who were going, were watching the tube when the news broke. You should have seen the reaction on their faces when they showed the National Guard shooting into the crowd. First the adam's apple went down with that big swallow of revelation, "that could have been us," then the revulsion---then the rage. What was our country coming to? There was a lot of big talk on campus, but very little action.

My response? --- I went hunting. I've had some of my best thoughts and ideas---even revelations while walking a field with a gun or sitting on the bank of a river or lake in the pursuit of fish. Wasn't it Henry David Thoreau who told us a man needs to be able to be alone with himself, a time to gather one's thoughts and weigh his feelings?

I did a lot of that---with a 16 gauge Remington model 870 pump shotgun that my father bought for me when I was eleven years old. When my mother dropped me off for school I had some pencils and paper, my clothes, my shotgun and some shells.

One of the "wunder kind" from up on the third floor of the dorm was watching me unload. When he saw my gun case, he yelled "no guns". I yelled back "shut up"! And went straight in to see the head resident, also a New Yorker, but must have been from upstate, because he didn't have the accent. I told him it was the fall semester and I planned to hunt. He told me he would keep my gun in his office and I could get it when needed.

So I picked up my gun and some shells and headed down the hill toward the bottoms. I had to walk through town to get there but that was no big deal. This is a small, rural Missouri town with a bank, dry-goods store, tavern, drugstore with a soda fountain and a feed store on the same street. So, seeing someone with a hunting vest on and carrying a gun didn't draw a second look. Of course you keep the breach open so they know it isn't loaded, which is proper firearms etiquette.

2. Up—Up and Away

The bottoms weren't far. I started working the higher ground parallel with the railroad tracks hoping to kick up some doves and look over the scenic bottoms at the same time. There was a peaceful serenity in that. The cares of the world seemed to disperse and fade away with the clouds.

The sound of a push cart on the tracks broke the tranquility of the moment. It was still quite a ways off so I sat down and waited for them to pass, seeing how I didn't have permission to hunt here. I watched them approach. They would stop here and there and spray certain plants, which didn't make sense to me. Why didn't they spray them all if they were near the tracks? The plants were tall, green and lush. I'd been walking through patches of them while I was hunting so I took a closer look. That's when the lightning struck and all the bells and whistles went off.

Hell, they were spraying weeds alright—it was WEED, Marijuana that is. I heard it was growing wild down here. They used to make rope out of it. Talk about getting my head straight—I'd have a little help now. So I moved up the hill high enough to be sure I was out of reach of the sprayer and started picking. I filled my game bag up on my vest and headed back toward school. I walked back through town and stopped at the ice-cream shop and had a shake.

You can smoke it while it's green like that but it takes a lot of matches—and you still get the munchies. The shake was great but it seemed the people were looking at me a little closer. My game bag didn't look like it was full of doves, but it was full. Maybe they could smell it? Or maybe it was my paranoia working on me.

I got back to school and dropped my gun off, went to my room and took the fourth drawer out of my bureau and filled it full of grass. It smelled for a few days while it was drying, like a fragrance from on high. Friends would come by and ask if I had any smoke and I'd say "check the fourth drawer in the dresser." And to see the look on their face when they opened the drawer! If I only knew about funniest home video's I could have paid my tuition.

At least now I was finally being accepted – partially— by New York and New Jersey.

~~~

I had a friend come from St.Louis on the train; we filled up two suitcases full of grass for his return. Another time friends came in a car and dropped us off in the bottoms with extra long trash bags. There was a full moon. Using the moonlight as a background—I could see the difference between the male and the female plants and I'd cut the females, hand them back to the guy behind me and he'd stick them into the trash bags. Then when we were ready we'd blink the flash light and the car would come and pick us up---just like in the movies. Trouble was—that weed wasn't very good. But it was a hell of a lot of fun.

3. Pick a Number

The lottery had put a lot of pressure on everyone. That night had a profound effect on a lot of people. At the end of the evening when it was clear who would go and who would stay, a number of guys went and sat in their rooms alone—The rest stayed up and partied.

There were a lot of questions. What were the conditions to be able to keep a II S deferment? What if you dropped a class or your grades were low? These were all critical issues. One stipulation that was quite clear was that you had to stay in school. No taking off a semester on some sabbatical or trying to make some money for tuition. If you did that, your II S would change to I A, making you fresh meat for the draft. That's T.S. or in Russian—tough shitsky. If your number was 195 or less, you might as well start packing your bags, because your chances of being called up were excellent. The year that corresponded to my birth, 1951, there were 551,806 young men drafted—the most in any year of the war!! So—everybody stayed in school. Oh, we had such an educated bunch in those years!!

At the first lottery my number was 347. But again, that number didn't count for me. It would be the next year for me. But I thought I was on a role. I didn't like the school and hated the people that attended. It was not the intellectual endeavor, nor the source of higher education I had hoped it would be. I'd heard stories of Canada and Europe and they were like pouring gasoline on a fire. They lit my interest and I wanted to see and experience a new world. This one---to me---was full of abuse and persecution.

You remember "Love America or leave it!" God I was tired of hearing that! No doubt I brought most of my problems upon myself, but I had had enough. My luck was good; I'd get a high number next time too. So I quit school and decided to go to Europe for a semester.

Great decision! My future was riding on a coin toss at the next lottery. That's why all life's major decisions should be made when you're eighteen---it's when you've got all the answers.

4. Up Against the Wall

I had to clear all my stuff out of the dorm and get it back to St. Louis. Jack was a Mid-westerner who lived on my floor in the dorm. He was short and rarely shaved. His black hair looked like he cut it himself and was never combed. But what bothered me---was the weaselly look he had---you just knew something was amiss with the guy. Maybe it was those dark, deep set eyes that were a little too close together. I needed a car and he had one. It was a 1958 Chevy Belair station wagon. A black and beat to shit rust bucket with bald tires and burned two quarts of oil every fifty miles. I figured it would get me to St. Louis. He wanted fifty bucks for the car. If I wanted the license plate it would be another ten spot. I told him to keep the plate –I'd take a chance. After all, I was planning to drive at night.

We made the deal. I gave him fifty bucks and he gave me the keys and two gallons of bulk oil and said "don't bother to check the oil-- every fifty miles just pour two quarts in." Nice guy, but he wouldn't let go of the license plate.

~~~~

Winfield was a black guy from St. Louis. I wished I had known him before because he was a good guy. I thought I was the only student from St. Louis. He was fed up with the school and was heading back home and needed a ride. We agreed I'd take him and his stuff home for twenty-five bucks and gas money.

When my roommate found out he asked "you really going to give that black guy a ride home?"

"Sure---his money's green. And besides, where's all that liberal bullshit I've been hearing all this time?" I wanted his company and needed his help with the cost. Winfield on the other hand, was not at all impressed with the car. It was indeed a junker. It had no license plate, and we'd soon find out it had no heat either.

We waited till rush hour to take off thinking we'd have a better chance getting through Kansas City without the plate. Every fifty miles we'd stop and add the oil. Two hundred miles—that's four stops. It was just before Christmas and it was cold---fifteen degrees and getting colder. If you think it wasn't—you stop in the flat lands in fifteen degree temperatures with a wind out of the north and pour in two quarts of oil that are as thick as molasses! Winfield would light matches and hold them under the steering wheel to help keep my hands from freezing.

There was so much blue smoke pouring out the back of the car I couldn't see out of the rear view mirror. We made it all the way across Missouri and into St. Charles County, just a few miles from St. Louis., when our luck ran out.

Within a two week period just prior to our arrival in St. Charles, there had been two policemen killed in routine traffic stops. They had no suspects and were looking hard to pin it on someone. There was a lot of fear out there. We'd soon see how much.

It happened like this: A cop pulls up behind us but I can't make him out from all the smoke coming out of the rear end---until he turns on his lights. I pull over, jump out and walk toward his car thinking it's better he doesn't see

Winfield and he can sit in his nice warm car and just maybe---maybe I can talk my way out of this.

He yells "Get back in the car, put your hands on the wheel and look forward."
This doesn't look good. Check this out: two guys, one white---one black, driving a junk car with no license plate and the back end is full of stereos, furniture, clothes, and my shotgun. What would you think?

The cop walks up to my door, the window is down and I look at him. But I don't see him. I'm looking down the barrel of his gun. I know something about guns---hunting and fishing you know. I can see the bullets in the cylinder and it looks like you could drop a dime down the barrel. It's a 44 magnum. I'm dealing with "Dirty Harry." Worse yet it's shaking. The gun's shaking. The cop is scared. I can hear it in his voice.

"Get out of the car—put your hands on your head—feet back—and lean against the car." I do it! He sticks the gun in my back and says "Move and I'll cut you in half."
I think to myself, oh Lord, don't let me have some involuntary reflex like a hick-up or a burp, not now, please! He frisks me for weapons. I start telling him our story but he's not listening. Back up comes—lots of it. They put us in separate cars and take us to the station.

Once we get to the station where they way out-number us, they start to relax and listen. Our student I.D.s' are valid. The semester is over and our story is starting to be plausible, except for the car. They can't believe the car story. "Nothing is stranger than the truth."

When I tell them the plate was going to cost an extra ten bucks, one guy rolls his eyes and another one starts laughing. A cop comes into the room and says he can't find any record of the car. No registration---no title, he says it must have been scrapped.

"That's what I'm going to do with it when I get our stuff home. I should get twenty- five bucks for it." I said. Another roll of the eyes.

We went through the story for the fifth time, it's always the same. But I can see they are starting to believe us. So I said "Guys, it's Christmas and it's getting late. Our parents are expecting us, what do we do now?"

It never ceases to amaze me. When you're eighteen, you're a big macho man to your friends till the cops got a gun in your face and it behooves you to be a kid again.

We wished each other Merry Christmas and they drove us back to the car and let us go. I had to promise to scrap the car when I got home. They didn't give me one ticket---not one! They just let us drive away. "Divine intervention?"

I had Winfield call his mom. She came and picked him up not far from their home. He was pissed because that wasn't our deal and it was inconvenient for her. But I was paranoid to drive through North St. Louis so late and in our circumstances. I was afraid St. Louis's finest might not be so understanding.

I brought his things to him the next day. That night I made it home without a problem. I kept the car for about two weeks. Had to dodge a couple of cops during that time and finally figured I'd pushed my luck far enough. I scrapped the car—got twenty-five bucks.

5. The Last Christmas

We had a nice Christmas. My middle brother was home—my oldest brother was in the navy in Vietnam and we missed him. But it was still nice. They were all nice, but they were never the same after my dad died. He died in mid January when I was thirteen years old. Every Christmas after that until my last one at home when I was eighteen, there was always a void. You never really talked about it—but it was always there.

I loved my mother. She did her best---and it was great. I remember years later apologizing to her for being such an ass and praying if I ever had kids that they wouldn't cause me as much pain and heartache as I caused her.

~~~~

Christmas was over and it was now mid January. Most of the kids going to school were back at it. I was at home on the couch watching TV. Now that might work at your house, but not at ours. My mom came home after work one day and I was on the couch eating ice cream and watching TV. She said "If you think you're going to sit around here and do nothing all day, you've got another think coming!" I said "No mom, I'm going to Europe, I'm just thinking how I'm going to raise some cash."
She probably thought 'yeah right' but said" Well, you better get at it." And I did.

The only thing I had of real value was motorcycle. It was an old 1954 650cc Triumph. I bought it in pieces from a friend named Lonnie who had a good business sense and was a mechanical wis. The year before he had been pushing it on me and I finally said, "If we can get it running I'll buy it". So we put it together in his basement and Lo and Behold –it ran!! We used an old lawn mower gas tank that held a quart of gas. It had straight pipes---no mufflers. It was bored and stroked---this bike would run. But it sure looked funny, especially with that little gas tank. They loved me at the pumps when I'd pull in for gas—time after time---fifteen cents please.

I did graduate up to a real gas tank—but still no mufflers or lights. She was strictly a daytime ride. I had an old German helmet and the license plate was on a sting that hung around my neck and down my back---just barely legal. But I got one ticket after another. I was in one municipal court on Wednesday in one town, Tuesday in another, Thursday in another, it finally came to the point where I just couldn't afford to stop anymore. Of course I knew all the neighborhoods so I could cut through yards, back alleys and behind buildings and was pretty successful. Till one day.

~~~~

There was about eight of us riding together. It had been raining for a solid week and this was the first day it was clear. Lonnie and I were in the lead. There was this long straight stretch---the kind that just begged you to open her up and stretch her out---and we did. Lonnie and I were way out in front and started slowing down to let the others catch up. It was great.

Then the wind started whistling through my helmet. I moved my head around but it didn't stop. That's no wind buddy, that's a siren. We both looked back and saw the cop gaining on us fast. We looked at each other and simultaneously down shifted and opened em up. Lonnie had a Sportster so he edged out ahead, which was good because he knew this area better than I did. We got to the top of the hill and cut through a construction site to get onto a new highway where we'd have been home free. But when we pulled into that construction area I knew we were done. It had been raining for a solid week and we sank up to our axles in mud. The cop pulled up and got out taking his time and casually beckoned to us with his index finger to come over to him. No where to run, no where to hide.

We had to work together on each bike to get them out of the mud---the cop is smiling all the time. Maybe this is good. No. We both got tickets for doing 90 in a 30.

"Hey kick it down a little—maybe to 40, you had some fun here too" I said to him. He admitted to finding the whole thing funny, but he said we were doing over 100 and he wasn't going to arrest us for trying to out run him. Nice guy!!

That was an expensive evening in court, plus a bonus. We had to go to driving school. "Familiarity breeds contempt" That's what I learned. And it actually helped me a couple of times later on.

~~~~

By now I was much too well known by the authorities and was continually being pulled over and hassled weather I had done anything wrong or not. It was a very frustrating time. There were a few guys that loved my bike so I was able to sell it for $650. That was the lion share of money for my trip. I worked when I could and was always good about saving money, so things were looking up. I had enough; at least it was all I was going to get.

6. A Connecticut Yankee

I had a friend from New Haven, Connecticut that I knew from college. We were going to travel to Europe together and had talked a lot about it at school. I called him and told him I'd be up to his place in a few days and we'd go. Great!

I said good bye to St Louis. It was a sad farewell with my Mom. I don't think she really thought I would go. But for the rest I could care less. I was burned off by school, I didn't seem to have any friends and there were the continual hassles from the law.

I took a flight to New York and a bus to New Haven, found my buddy's house and knocked on the door. He lived in an old suburban neighborhood, in a big house with dormers and large overhangs. There was six inches of snow on the ground and it was still snowing and felt a lot colder than it was.

He answered the door and I said "Hey Man." He had some 'whipped—whoosie' look on his face and said "I can't go." Shit! I don't believe this. "What do you mean?" He gave some lame excuse, but after talking with him for awhile I knew he never had any intention of going on the trip. So all the talk at school about going to Europe was bullshit—a game to him. To me it was real.

I called my mother that night and told her the story. She said "Well son, do you want to come home?"
I looked outside and the weather was depressing to say nothing about how I felt about this guy stringing me along. And I must admit, the thought of going home did cross my

mind. But I said "no." I've come this far and I'm not going to quit now. I'm going to keep on going. Besides, I didn't think there was much back in St. Louis for me anyway.

~~~~

I took a bus early the next morning to JFK airport. When I got there it was still snowing---another grey winter day. It was gloomy, and I was too. I thought I would have some company but that was not to be the case. So I hunted down the Icelandic Airlines counter and bought a round trip ticket good for six months from New York to Luxembourg to New York for $180. How'd you like to do that today?

I picked up my ticket and headed for the gate. What a surprise! When I got there the gate area was full of young people---mostly college kids. I didn't see one old person and only a few straight people, mostly long hairs, freaks, and hippie types, all with the same ideas that I had. I could blend in here nicely. This was going to be a good trip!

Icelandic Airlines was a start up company at the time. They found their niche in hauling kids mostly, between Europe and the states. As time went on it became clear why there wasn't any old people on this flight, and certainly no business people. A normal flight took about six to seven hours to Europe. Icelandic was going to take thirteen---with a stop over in Iceland for fuel!!! No, we weren't on a jet. Icelandic was flying old constellations still painted that military grayish green with four Pratt and Whitney radial propeller engines.

I probably flew on one of the last commercial Trans Atlantic flights on a propeller driven aircraft.

Our flight was full. Seems there was some story about a prior flight that while on take off a rear window blew out. I can't confirm that, nor did I really care. I had a seat on this flight and I was going. Everybody's bullet proof when they're eighteen!

I had a window seat. When we took off I was looking out over the wing and watching the props spin. I swear when we lifted off that wing flapped. I looked across the isle and through the other window and that one was too. Now it wasn't flapping like a bird, but it was moving a good foot to foot and a half. It gave me a new meaning for fixed winged aircraft! When we cleared the ground everyone on board started cheering and applauding—no wonder. It was exhilarating.

These beautiful Icelandic girls who were our flight attendants appeared. Every young mans' dream. Long blonde hair and blue eyes--- positively stunning! A figment of my imagination was coming true. And they were walking up and down the isle with a cart full of booze---and the booze was free! Something about accommodating us for the long flight, an excellent business practice.

I was in love before we got to Iceland. And so drunk when we landed in Luxembourg I thought it was a city in France. I knew I was going to like Europe.

7. First Day in the "Old World"

Somehow I made it through customs and into the city. A lot of people were talking about going to the Youth Hostel so I kind of tagged along. That's where I met a Canadian guy named Jeff. Long and lanky with curly blonde hair past his ears; he was going back to Red Deer, Alberta---Red Deer; hell, even the names of the cities in Canada sounded wild. I knew I'd get there one day.

Jeff was going to head back to Canada the next day. He had a nice piece of hash he wasn't going to take along. so we decided to smoke it up---of course.

There was a tunnel in the mountain across the valley where the trains were passing through. We had to cross the valley on the tracks—no pedestrian walkway. No problem getting there and getting a good buzz on. It was on the way back, about half way across the valley a train was coming. No sweat, we just crossed over to the next track. Then another train comes out of the tunnel and is heading straight for us.

Damn! There's no way we can make it off the bridge in time and it's too high to jump. I'm watching this big ass freight train bearing down on us fast and I'm standing there like a deer in the headlights when Jeff grabs my arm and swings me onto a platform about two feet wide and five feet long that's hanging out past the bridge. It's the safety box for the workers if this situation happens to them. What a rush!! The trains didn't kill us, but they sure killed our buzz. I haven't been in Europe a day and was almost toast.

We got the hell off that bridge and fired up another number and tried to make light of the matter. It worked. What helped also was that I went into a little shop and bought a bottle of wine. What a pleasure, not having to lie about my age. Hell, there were people my age dying in Vietnam right now and if they did make it home they couldn't buy a beer in a bar. Something's wrong with that picture.

We opened the wine and drank it while we were walking down the street. Well, that one led to another and pretty soon we're cruising along feeling no pain. We start to pass this old stone castle type structure with a high tower and only one window that's near the top. Jeff stops me, cups his hands over his mouth and yells up at the window "Rapunzel Rapunzel---let down your golden hair." I'm rolling on the ground laughing. I almost broke the bottle of wine. It fit so perfectly—the tower and all. If that window would have opened, it would have pushed me over the edge.

My mother used to read that ferry tale to me and I loved to look at the picture of the tower. It hit me; I was in Never Never Land and loving it. Damn, what a great first day.

8. All That Glitters---

Youth Hostels were great for meeting other travelers and finding out information on the places you wanted to see, what to do and what not to do. But once I found out such knowledge I found I could do better on my own. It's a great 'starter package' so to speak.

Jeff and I made it back to the Youth Hostel just before they locked up. That's where I met Rebecca. A pretty California girl with long brown hair cascading down her back and a shapely figure that would turn any mans'eye. She was going South to get away from the cold and that was my plan too. It's cold in Northern Europe in February. We decided to hitch-hike South together. She was leery of going alone and I reinforced her fears because I thought with this "Hotty" I wouldn't be standing on the side of the road for long. We had heard the hitch-hiking was slow in Luxembourg and slower yet in France and Spain. But at least the trains were cheap in Spain. Course there was a reason for that—you could walk about as fast as some of them.

   The plan was to meet after breakfast out on the road in front of the Youth Hostel. So I'm standing by the side of the road to Metz and Nancy and here she comes. What the hell!! She's got some goofy looking cowboy hat on with her beautiful long hair rolled up and tucked away underneath. Her large blue checked flannel shirt and baggy jeans are hiding all her beautiful assets.

"What are you dressed like this for? The whole idea is to catch these truckers eyes and get them to stop, because they're sure not looking at me."

She got pissed at my chauvinistic platitudes. But "Hey" So we stood by the road and watched everyone pass us by for about an hour.

"That's it for me." I said "You either go in there, pointing to the restaurant, and make yourself look beautiful or I'm out of here. I can do better on my own than trying to hitch-hike with another guy."

You always do better alone. People are afraid of picking up two people unless they're a couple. And if we were a couple---that's not the kind these people wanted to pick up.

She went in and made the change. Came out and looked great, five minutes later we are in a truck heading for Metz. I wanted to say "I told you so." But didn't because I knew we were done before we started. No use beating a dead horse. Once again the old cliché comes to mind---"All that glitters is not gold."

~~~

The next morning I took a train through France to Figueres, just on the Spanish side of the border. Ahhh, sunny Spain, and it was too, at least today. And warmer too, not quite as warm as I had hoped---but it was great? I was in much better spirits as I walked out of the station and asked where the "careterra" ---the road--- to Barcelona was.

Yeah, I could speak a little Spanish. After all, I took two years of it in high school, but like everybody else it was only as a prerequisite to get to college. So there was no big incentive to really learn the language. "Boy you better listen up and study harder" I can just hear the "I told ya so" jerks. But I'm here and they're there. And damn it, "I told YOU so!"

I could get my point across and knew my vocabulary would get better by the moment. But understanding their replies, now that was a whole different ball game. I had just come through Luxembourg and France where I couldn't understand a word. Now I was in Catalan where proper Spanish is spoken with a lisp. Something to do with Louis XIV, we have to mimic the king ya know! My Thpanith ith pith poor at betht and now I have to thpeak it with an accent like I'm gay. Is there no justice? I love it.

It was an early spring and the flowers and bushes were blooming. The fragrance of spring was in the air making the perception of being a free man in a free world almost tangible. I was walking down the road to Barcelona---the next city on the map---with some 'coin of the realm' in my jeans and not a care in the world. We hicks and hayseeds would say---"It don't get no better."

Everybody was right. The hitch-hiking wasn't very good at all in Spain. Mind you, my surroundings were picturesque, but my patience was growing thin. And I could use a drink. I had a glass of wine at the station before I left---only three pesetas, or about a nickel, for a glass of win--- in a bar. I like that.

The sun was high in the sky and its full force of heat for the day was right now. I'd been on the road for about three hours and not a single ride. Then I spied a little sign tacked on a tree just high enough to be out of reach. It said just what I wanted it to say.

"BAR 3 KILOMETERS."

I did a rough calculation from metric and figured I could make it. Seemed like a long mile and three quarters, but as I came around the bend---there it was, my oasis. As I drew nearer my elation started to sink. No! This couldn't be! The damn place was closed! There wasn't a single person in sight. Now I'm pissed. That last stretch was a long one and I was never a very good walker. Hey, I'm American; we fight for the closest parking spot to the door. This walking business is about as foreign to me as Spain is. I thought if I had a match this place would never deceive another weary traveler.

Just then a car comes into sight. They aren't slowing down either but as they pass I see a green rectangular plate like in the states and it says USA up in the corner. I start yelling and jumping up and down and waving my arms saying "That's me, I'm American. That's me!!" I can see the guy is looking in his rear view mirror and his break lights go on. Haleluya!! He's stopping. I go running up to the car and he says "I thought I'd better stop because it looked like you were loosing it." He didn't know how close to the truth he was. He asked me where I was going and I say with as much of a calm demeanor as I can fake "Barcelona."

"Your in luck, we can take you there."

He's an American GI stationed in Germany. He and his wife are on holiday in Spain for a week. He tells me all the green plates I'll see on cars are owned by GI's---a good thing to know.

I'm riding in a 1965 Plymouth Valiant all the way to Barcelona. What a relief. But I figure it's trains from here on out in Spain. Patience level has always been low.

We pulled into Barcelona just as the sun was going down.

~~~~

It doesn't matter if you're in the country or the city when the sun goes down – that period known as dusk has a bizarre feel to it. Like a changing of the guard or changing of realms. Especially when you're in a new world where you can't speak the language, have no idea where you're going, where to eat, or where to spend the night. The darker it gets the more pressing those issues become. Alcohol and smoke may lessen their effect, but they're there just the same.

They asked me where I was going in the city. I told them I had no idea. So they dropped me off at the lower end of the Ramblas, where a statue of Columbus looks out to sea on top of a tall pedestal in the center of a huge traffic circle. It was from Barcelona that he left on his voyage to the "New World".

This is the "happening" area with people and cars everywhere. Some parked on sidewalks, others jostling and honking as in some private oblivion with no regard to the lines on the streets. The people dodging in and out of the way on their own mission of importance. It's a controlled chaos. I'm digging it. Beats the hell out of "get in line boy" "You rolled that sign back there son; I'm going to have to give you a ticket."

Really?---Stick it---pig. I'm free in Franco's Spain. Sad commentary on the US.

The Ramblas is the spot. Everything's going on at once. Move up the street and the scene changes but not the pace of the action. The shops are full and lively as are the restaurants and small cafes. You can hear the laughing and loud retorts back and forth. The people are watching and listening, especially the Guardia Seville. Others in the shadows with that predator look and to them you're just another piece of meat. Maybe an easy one since you're a foreign kid. You're rich to them, yeah really, maybe not back home but here you are. My dollar was worth sixty pesetas. A glass of wine was a nickel, a beer was a dime, ten for a dollar. But could you have just one? Not I. Ha ha.

9. The Key

I needed a place to stay so I started asking around and met a Dutch guy named Adje [odd-jay]. He told me he was staying in a pension down by the port called the "Pension Clave." The 'Key'.

There were no Youth Hostels to speak of. The lower strata of society and the young travelers looking for a cheap place to stay sought out pensions. They were usually small, private, cheap hotels with a lot less amenities. I went down with Adje and knocked on the door. It was huge by American standards. An old lady opened up wearing the traditional all black dress. Told her I was looking for a room and she showed us in.

The room was rather dark and dingy. Everything seemed grey, the sheets as well. It had a high ceiling with a plaster motif around the light fixture which was a metal rod hanging down from the ceiling with a single low wattage light bulb at the end. The toilet was down the hall. Pull the chain. No window. Same light fixture. I don't know if the musty smell was from the high humidity or the last occupant. That really didn't bother me, it was just a place to sleep and by the time I was in need of that –it wouldn't matter anyway.

~~~

I stayed in Barcelona for awhile. The first real European city I ever got to know. First city anywhere really. I met some very interesting people here, especially for a kid from St Louis.

There was a small plaza about two blocks off the Ramblas that had a mom and pop restaurant with fantastic paella, a saffron-seafood rice dish, and was cheap to boot. Just eighty cents US for a big plate with bread and a glass of wine. I was a regular! It's the place where I saw Ben Cartwright speaking Spanish on TV, Hoss as well, and he had the lisp down pat. Life is full of wonders.

I came out of the restaurant one day, stuffed to the gills, and sat down in the sunshine. Across the plaza were two guys. Both had long blonde hair, one was a head taller than the other. The tall one had a leather head band; the short one had a three inch wide leather belt on the outside of his shirt with a coin purse with strings holding it to his belt. They had peasant shirts open in the front and corduroy pants. I knew right away they weren't Americans; otherwise they would've had jeans and a jean shirt. That was the uniform.

We made eye contact and started walking toward each other. The tall one asks "you American?" I said "Yeah, from St. Louis, Mo."

"That's in the middle of the country isn't it?'

"Yes it is."

"We're Danes from Copenhagen."

Ya know, we have the best education in the world but damned if I knew where Copenhagen was in Denmark!! So I shut up and tried to look wise. We hung around together for awhile. So these were Viking's I thought. They could drink and party that's for sure. I told them I was going to Ibiza which is one of the Balearic Islands off the coast from Valencia. There are a bunch of freaks living there, and on Formentera they were living in caves. Adje and I were leaving the next day. Why don't you come along? They thought that a good idea.

    We met later that night at our pension. Adje was there with his twelve string guitar and a bunch of other people we'd met that day. All of them heading for the boat to Ibiza tomorrow. We drank, sang, smoked and partied till I don't know when, but there was always some fear when it came to catching a buzz, seemed like nobody wanted to spend any time in one of Franco's jails.

10. The Boat to Ibitha

There was time enough to shop before the boat left. Our fourth class tickets did not include lunch; so everybody bought bread, cheese, sausage and wine—lots of it. The boat was supposed to leave at noon but didn't. No word as to why, so while we waited we started eating and drinking. We consumed everything! Then word came down that the weather was rough and that was the hold up, so we'd be leaving shortly.

Rough was putting it mildly. When we got out of the port into open water there was a full gale blowing. The boat was bobbing around like a cork and it wasn't long before people were seeing their lunches again. Most everybody but the crew was sick. People were puking their guts out all over the boat. Nice.

I wasn't sick yet but knew it wasn't far off. Our tickets were for out on the deck only. So not only was everybody sick, they were getting soaked by the sea spray as well. I started trying cabin doors until I found one that was open. When I did, I crawled into an upper bunk that wasn't occupied. The guy below me was making moaning and groaning sounds like he was in the throws of death. He probably felt like. I laid there with my eyes closed and everything spinning. I didn't puke but I was sure sick.

Finally the boat docked on the leeward side of the island and we could get off. The passengers were greener than the island itself. It wasn't as tropical as I had hoped. No big coconut palms swaying in the breeze hanging over the white sand beaches. I learned later I was in the wrong latitude for that, but, if you're going to dream…

It was more arid, with smaller trees, bushes, and cactus. Everything was starting to bloom and give off that Garden of Eden look. Everywhere buds were breaking forth and the fragrance of those in full bloom was what perfumer's have been seeking since day one. What a nice reprieve from the cold up North. This year in particular because so many said it was much colder than usual---a record breaker.

~~~

We swaggered up to the nearest café and I got a café con leche and a croissant. Nothing too heavy just yet, much too soon for that and I was still trying to get my wits about me. Things were still spinning a bit.

Some guys were talking about getting a house to rent. Fill it up with people so it would be affordable. It sounded like a good idea, so I tagged along to see. We found a house about a mile from town. It was nice enough. Concrete block like all the rest, but not painted up as pretty. It had multi levels like there had been a lot of additions put on without a lot of planning or the use of a level.

The house was unfurnished and had no hot water, none of which bothered me. What did bother me was the two New Yorkers who tried to run the show. The guy was tall. His black dirty hair hung down to his shoulders. His hand kept moving his bangs off his pimply forehead. This guy was so skinny, he'd have to run around in the shower to get wet. His jeans were too big to fit him and he had to put extra holes in his belt to make it tight enough to hold things up; leaving too much belt that hung down past his crotch. But he was cool—right? His wife was huge. She was as wide as she was tall; with that Momma Cass look---only she was a bitch.

Now let's be clear here. I know this sounds judge mental and it is. But I had been crapped on for a full semester by assholes like these and I was done with that. And these two were even worse, arrogant slobs that knew better than their European hosts. They pissed me right off.

> (*Now--- I do need to make a disclaimer here. You judge a person by their deeds and actions-- their heart so to speak, not their looks. I've been a little hard on these two especially and New York in general. When my wife and I were doing the Great Circle in our boat, we pulled in to New York City and had a wonderful time. We loved the city and met nothing but nice friendly people everywhere we went. They should send some of the nice one's out to Park College! And take the assholes—oops— that I met and put them on a trash barge and take them out to sea.*)

These two were really obnoxious. They played some kind of intellectual game as if they were deep thinkers, referring to Nietzshe and Kaufka and oops there's Karl Marx again. I waited until a deep thought had grasped everyone's attention and the room was silent and called out.

"Hey, could any of those guys catch fish?"

Everybody turned and looked. The stare from the New York elites was nothing new; I'd seen that for the last six months. "You stupid Hoosier!"

I followed that up with "I met some fishermen, they said the 'blues' were running and gave me ten of them that we can have for dinner—look! and held the fish up." The 'Euros' were delighted.

I couldn't help myself. I had to take it one more step. "You all—meaning the New Yorkers—they love that 'you all' ya know!—ever get out and meet any of the locals here? See how they're living and what they're doing to make a living instead of talking about a bunch of dead intellectuals? Oh yeah,---I met an old lady on the way back from the docks and when she saw the fish, she told me a good recipe on how to cook them, so we're all set for dinner."

The Euros loved me---and I loved them too. But I didn't come this far to play games with assholes from the States. I came on this trip to see and experience new cultures and ideas; to meet the people and see their lifestyles, to see the sights and drink the drinks and eat the foods. And I was drinking it in with intoxicating intemperance!!

~~~~

Formentera was the other Balearic Island I planned on going to. I was in town talking to different travelers who had been there and some who were going. They said it was a cool place to go and see. That the people living in the caves were mostly Americans and the islanders didn't really like them. I didn't think I would either. So I bought a ticket back to Barcelona on the next boat. I said good bye to Adje and left. I didn't know it then of course, but I'd be seeing Adje again.

I'd about had it with my fellow countrymen. Looking back, I think it was from this point on that I steered clear of them.

I took the same boat back to Barcelona. The seas were calm, the water a deep blue and with a few puffy clouds over head, it made for a lovely cruise. Especially when compared to what we faced coming out. It took half as long to get there too.

11. Back in Barcelona

I went back to the Pension Clave, knocked on the huge door and the old lady welcomed me in. She still had that black mourning outfit on. I wanted to put my arm around her shoulder and say "Hey, its okay. There's a life out there to be lived." But who was I to interfere in her way of life.

Barcelona was alive. I frequented a lot of bars in the lower quarters where drinks were cheap, the air was thick with smoke and the stench of stale beer and wine was inbedded in the floors and furniture. This contrasted and battled the aroma of the sausages and hams hanging from the rafters just above your head. The winner depended on where your head was.

Sawdust was scattered over the floor to soak up what ever dropped from the bar or the patrons leaning against it. This is where I was introduced to Tapas. Those small plates loaded with culinary delights like squid and tripe [avoid] and nuts, olives—more kinds than I knew ever existed. And the best—cured Spanish ham. Lots of little things I'd never heard of all rolled up and fastened together with toothpicks—hence the sawdust. That's where the toothpicks and olive pits and you don't want to know what else ends up. And believe me –you don't want to end up down there either.

But how civilized!! To drink and to nibble on little delicacies, turn your head and spit out an olive pit or a piece of sausage that tasted like it might be off. Ya gotta love it. I sure did. There's a sense of freedom in that. And until you've experienced it, you can't really appreciate it. Ready everybody------SPIT----Ya see! It was all nicely swept out every night and clean sawdust scattered around in the morning for a new day.

The people I'd meet in such places were generally friendly and open and always interesting. And when I'd come in alone somebody would always wave me over and we'd have a few drinks. They'd want to know my story, then they'd tell me theirs. Before the end of the night they would surely tell me of the fascinating and beautiful things in their city. What to see and what not to see and when best to do it. They were a treasure trove of knowledge. One that I would seek out in every country I'd visit.

It was in these kinds of places that I would find out how to get around the lines at the front doors of museums, or the door where no one was collecting tickets; the places of beauty that weren't written about in "Europe on $5.00 a day." This was why I was here. This was truly experiencing the culture of the people.

It was in these places that I would here the soft conversations—the whispers of discontent with the Franco Regime. The sense of fear during such conversations was nearly tangible. There was a lot of anger and frustration. No one wanted to end up in Franco's jails. It was easy to get in, but hard to get out.

His right arm of terror was the Guardia Seville. During the civil war literally thousands of people would be picked up and never heard from again. And they were ever present. Every major intersection or suspected area that insurrection might spring up---the Guardia were there.

They were easy to see, with their immaculate green uniforms and signature patent leather hats folded like a tricorn. They'd be on the corners with their arms resting on their machineguns on slings over their shoulders---the barrels pointing at the pedestrians as they walked by. You think that's not intimidating? I don't mind cops with automatic weapons, just don't point them at me! Back home I had the crap slapped out of me a few times by the cops. Here you were lucky if that's all that happened.

I met a Norwegian merchant marine in a bar and he told me a story about him and another sailor. They were having a big time in Barcelona, whoring and drinking and were severely loaded when his friend had to take a piss. Being drunk and late at night he just whipped it out and pissed on a post. Now normally that would be no big deal, even for the Guardia. Trouble was the post had a picture of Franco pasted onto it. They grabbed him, beat the shit out of him and put him in jail. He missed his ship. On their return trip they stopped again in Barcelona and the police released him back to the ship. Two months later! His friend wouldn't sign on to another ship that stopped in Spain.

~~~

I had a run in with the Guardia later on. Thank God it was aboard a ship or I still might be there. Formidable and intimidating—no question about it, that's fascism.

I saw people begging in the streets---another first for me. They were poorly clothed and dirty, sitting in places where the pedestrian traffic was higher so it might be more lucrative. Others with poorly wrapped bandages—dirty and in need of being changed, obviously not applied in a hospital. Still others in need of medical treatment and again, obviously going without.

Another shocker was a plaque I saw on the wall of the vestibule in the main cathedral. It was a list of the top hundred or so contributors in order or their generosity. I can just imagine the sacrifice one would make to get one's name a little higher up on the list. And who was to benefit?

How the people must have suffered during those years. But not all!! There is always those who prosper under any regime and fight any change to the status quo.

When Franco died the people elected a left of center candidate named Carreo Blanco. In of a year's time, I saw none of the aforementioned atrocities or abuses.

~~~~

It was about 10:00 PM. I saw at the top of a high hill near the port, what seemed to be a sporting event because of all the light that was beaming up into the sky. I went closer to see and there was a gate and a guard and only luxurious cars were allowed to enter. This certainly precluded me. But my curiosity had been aroused and I wanted to see what was up! There was a chain link fence about six feet high—no barb wire on top.

I have yet to see a fence I couldn't climb. So up and over I go. As I work my way up the hill I can here shots being fired. Now I've got to check this out. Every now and then a pigeon would fly by and I'd wonder what was making them fly at night? As I approached the crest of the hill and peered over I saw it was a shooting range. Immaculately cared for, well lit, and all stations facing the port so all the lead would fall on the slope of the hill toward the sea. Where the trap houses should have been—that's where the machines throw out clay discs called clay pigeons—were small wire cages with live pigeons in them. At the right time the cages would open and one or two pigeons would fly out and take their chances against the shooter. These guys were shooting live pigeons. Now I'm a Missouri boy and I've shot a lot of clay pigeons and quite a few live pigeons but I'd never seen an organized shoot with live pigeons. It was fascinating. That's why I saw the pigeons flying by while I was climbing up the hill.

I was watching and wondering at the same time how I might get involved. These shooters had all the right clothes and some high dollar guns but they really weren't knocking many of them down. It's the same all over. The gun's only as good as the guy behind it. That's when I heard the whistle,---then another. I saw two guards pointing at me and high stepping it my way. I turned around---hauled ass down the hill and cleared that fence a lot faster the second time than I did the first and set about blending into the crowd. I guess I'll come back when I can drive my Mercedes up to the gate---yeah, right!

12. Further South

Time too move on. I love Barcelona but the weather's still a bit cold. I wanted to experience some heat—tropical heat. Not this low 70's in the day time and high 30's at night. I met a couple of Dutch guys who were on their way back from the Canary Islands. They said it was hot down there and the beer was cold and there were a lot of beautiful girls from Northern Europe on the beaches. Sounded like "just the ticket" to me!! And that's just what I needed—a ticket. I could take a ship out of Barcelona or take a train across Spain diagonally to Cadiz and take the ship from there. It was cheaper that way and I could see the Spanish countryside. So that was it.

I headed down to the train station, checked the schedule and saw there was a train leaving at 2:30 heading south. If I could get a ticket there'd be time to go back to the pension, get my stuff and still make the train. Trouble was there was a hellish long line at the ticket window. Why the hell didn't they open another ticket window? There were four or five of them closed—it would have made a big difference in the line!

'Patience son, patience'! I've heard it all my life. And I can be patient at times---if there's a reason,--but damn. Truth be known there's rarely a sufficient reason in my book. And this didn't look like one now.

The line was moving, but so was the sun and with either one it's damn hard to tell. But I waited, I was good. It's getting close to noon, but I can still make it. The guy in front of me gets his ticket and steps aside. I step up to the window and the man behind the glass stands up and puts a 'Cerrado' sign over the window [CLOSED]. They're closed for siesta!

"BULLSHIT!!" I say! And start banging on the glass and yelling. Visions of that closed bar on the road that I had walked to start flashing through my mind and I really start to flip out. This isn't only about the ticket, there's vengeance involved here too.   Everybody starts backing away from me and I can see fear in their eyes. And rightly so!   In my mind I've been wronged and justice will rule out! The guy behind the window comes back and sells me a ticket. He's pissed off as well and saying something I can't make out, but I don't have too. It's not hard to imagine. I pick up my ticket and as I walk away I glance at the clock on the wall. It's straight up noon. I was right. But it doesn't matter. Everyone's looking at me with disdain, like I'm a wild and crazy foreigner and they're right. I feel like an ass and promise myself it will never happen again but I know deep down inside it will. Don't you laugh!!! We all have some character flaws,---I just have a few more than most.

~~~

There's a big difference between an express train and an inner city train, commonly known as a 'stop' train. The express goes from major city to major city. It's the fastest and most efficient, but at this time in Spain it's still not worth writing home about!   The 'stop' train on the other hand stops at every little town and village along the way. Hell, it can stop where there's no town at all! Guess which ticket I bought?!! Yep! If I'd have gone back to the pension, taken a nap and came back after siesta, bought a ticket on the express train, I'd have gotten to Madrid at the same time. Maybe this is some kind of righteous justice for the scene I made at the ticket window. It's all part of the education.

All is not lost though, because I boarded the train with a case of beer and a packet of Dormidinos. I was told they are sold as a sleep aid but are really a pretty heavy downer. So---after a couple of those and a few beers, I won't care where I am or when the train arrives. I wanted to see the Spanish countryside alright,---but I was going slow enough to study it. It wasn't long before the beers ran out and I'd have to get off to get a beer or wine at the station in the little kiosk---if there was one.

We're about three quarters of the way to Madrid when the train stops. I get off and get in line. The guy behind me says "Your train's leaving."

"No sweat, I can run faster than that train's going"

When I get my beer, I start running down the platform to the train. I'm catching up to it easily when I notice I'm about to run out of platform at the station. So I sprint the last few yards and jump, catch the rail, and swing myself onto the last car. Beer in hand! I look back at the station and the passengers on the platform were waving, cheering and laughing. I raised my beer in a salute. It was a good laugh and helped to break up the monotony.

When I got to Madrid I switched to the express train to Cadiz---much, much nicer.

13. The Port and a Ship South

Cadiz is a port on the south coast of Spain. It has a vibrant fishing industry and a lot of freight passing through it. The fish market was in the wee hours of the morning. They'd pull their boats up to the docks and haul their catch up to a wharf were it was laid out on trays, sold and shipped all over the world. Lot's of action—stay out of the way! It can run smooth or run rough and be dangerous depending on the weather. The people vary in size shape and color as much as the fish. They're always interesting.

The town had a lot of small shops, bars, restaurants, and cafes where it was easy to meet fellow travelers and interesting locals. Siesta was a time for the locals to gather at home. Schools would close and kids would come home. All commerce would cease as parents and family would gather together for the big noon day meal and fellowship with a time of relaxation after. What a great idea. It strengthens the family bonds and places the family in its proper perspective in life. Unless you're a big corporation where time is money and money is god.

It was during siesta, when the town was 'dead' and the streets deserted, except for the foreigners and a few stray dogs; that's when I met a group of young people heading for the Canaries. They were on the dock waiting for the ship with no where to go but lots to do. They were from all over. There were Dutch, always some Dutch guys, it doesn't matter where you go or how far off the road in some back woods lost place, if there's another foreigner there, the chances are they're Dutch.

There were Germans, French, Italians, Swedes, and Danes and then some---all waiting for the boat---playing guitars with harmonicas and flutes accompanying. Some singing, some dancing, some drinking wine, eating cheese, sausage and bread, fruit and citrus, and most all smoking hash. Most had long hair but others short.

Clothes varied like a gypsy dance troop. There were leather head bands, head scarves, arm bands, waist bands, in boots and sandals, or just plain barefoot. A true mélange of young people with one sure thing in common. They weren't 'In Line' and wanted no part of the 'Main Stream'. And I didn't either!

There were those in search and others in a lurch---running from someone or something. Yet others on some kind of fling, and that was really more my thing. School was in session. Everything was new here. I had heard of such travels and now I was experiencing them. I loved it.

I had a ticket for the boat in hand. So for me it was all sunshine and blue skies—light winds and no bugs! I had some 'coin of the realm' in my jeans and a secure place to sleep for the next three days. Life was good. Where I come from we'd say "It don't get no better."

I met a French couple from Marseille that told me to buy a 3rd or 4th class ticket for the boat. Once we get under way, then get your stuff and move up to second class and find an empty bunk. And that's what I did.

The accommodations, even in 2nd class weren't luxurious by any stretch but they were the best I'd had since leaving home. Everything was white with a fresh coat of paint. Even the sheets were white. And the shower

never ran out of hot water. I know—I stayed in it for over an hour.
I should have brought more food and drink along because they charged a premium aboard ship. I wouldn't get caught like that again. There was plenty of smoke—and smoke we did. We'd gather in the bow or on the fantail depending on the wind. But ever wary for to be jailed in Spain meant certain pain.

~~~~

Our ship came in. She off loaded her passengers and what freight she had. Mostly green bananas and some barrels of fish. When the last of the freight and all the passengers were aboard, she fueled up and was ready for the return voyage. We cast off our lines and headed South, to skirt the coast of Africa and then down to the Canaries. Passing near Gibraltar we hit a storm. Strong currents and high winds are notorious around Gibraltar and this storm was no exception. The ship was heaving to and fro while the crew was busy lashing down everything that was loose. Once again most everyone were sick aboard. Everywhere you went was the permeating nauseous smell of vomit.

The storm lasted through out the night and subsided by morning so that the weather was calm and clear as if nothing had happened the night before. Ah, but that smell was a dead give away. The weather remained calm the rest of the cruise---thankfully. But you knew after such an event she could kick your ass any time she wanted.

It's one thing to run into your house and down the basement during a storm, but at sea there's nowhere to run. Next time you here the weather man say "It's all clear, the storm has gone out to sea." Think about those sailors aboard the ships and how "Clear" it is for them.

When we entered the break waters of the port of Las Palmas on the Island Gran Canaria, the water was flat calm, not even a breeze. The ship stopped and dropped her anchor in the port.

"What's this" was the general cry from the passengers seeing how we could see the dock we were supposed to tie up to.

The ship's crew was going to have a fire drill. They lowered all the life boats and started all their motors. Trouble was, over half the life boats could not be lowered. Either one side or the other of the lowering wenches wouldn't work or wouldn't work in tandem, so that the life boats were all askew hanging lopsided to the bow or to the stern. Of the few boats that did make their launch only two could start their motors. I had the feeling that one of those would have been the captains' life boat.

And this was at flat calm---in the port for crying out loud. What would have happened if we would have had to abandon ship in that storm we went through? It didn't exactly inspire confidence in our crew or the ship for that matter. Mind you the ship always does much better than her passengers.

Las Palmas was beautiful. I finally made it to the heat. The water was a deep blue and the surf was invigorating. The beaches were full of tourists from all over North Europe. There were signs in every language with a heavy bent toward the Skandinavians. The local economy was thriving on the tourists. Now, I've heard a 'rule of thumb' that applies to those who go topless. The women who do aren't usually worth looking at. Not so here. These were some fine specimens. The locals weren't at all happy about it because of their strong catholic culture. But I wasn't complaining.

Another big plus—Alcohol was even cheaper here. Las Palmas is a tax free port. So quarts of name brand liquors were as little as two dollars a bottle. The Swedes were paying over twenty five dollars a bottle in Sweden. Denmark wasn't any cheaper. So every week there would be at least two Skandinavians who would drink themselves to death from alcohol poisoning.

With all this money rolling in with the tourists from up North, it's no wonder everything else was expensive. Places to stay were high and hard to find. Food, beer and wine in a café were higher as well. Ya gotta pay for that sunshine and beach.

14. The Canaries

I met a Canadian guy named Aiden from Moosejaw, Saskatchewan---Moosejaw, damn! Canada is supposed to be wild and all,--- but Moosejaw?

We were on the beach taking in the scenery. As the sun was going down and the temperature dropping a little bit, the tops and cover-ups were going on and the blue eyed beauties were heading back to their hotels. It was time for a change for us too, so we went to a local bar not frequented by many tourists. That's where I met Aalborg.

That's not some guy, it's Danish snapps, or akvavit,--- 40% fun—60% regrets. There's a guy in that bottle somewhere with a club and when you least expect it he'll whack you in the head. At that point you'll do something stupid that others will laugh at and maybe encourage---or if you're lucky you'll wake up and remember nothing---but the clubbing.

The sun was long gone and getting later. Aiden had the idea of sleeping on the beach because he was getting low on funds, and I'm always keen to save where I can. Why not? Going to sleep with the surf pounding in the back ground sounded good to me.

During the night I had some kind of dream or blurred vision of people standing around us but couldn't tell if it was real or not. Because by the time I went to sleep I had quite a glow going. Come morning—sure enough, Aiden had been robbed. They cut his sleeping bag at the bottom and stole his passport and what little money he did have. They didn't rob me, must have been because I woke up.

That put us in a foul mood,---either that or it was the hangover from the snapps.

I bought Aiden breakfast. It was the usual. Churros, a batter that came out of a machine in a long tubular shape, deep fried to a golden brown, then pulled out and snipped into manageable bites and sprinkled with sugar. Delicious! Churros and a café con leche. The sun was rising and so were our spirits. Aiden headed off to the Canadian Consulate. I saw him the next day and he had a new passport and a ticket to Moosejaw. I heard of my fellow countrymen waiting for as long as two or three weeks for a passport and forget about the ticket home.

~~~~

La Gran Canaria, is an island with lots of beaches, including Las Cantaras; a wide expanse of sand with a volcanic reef off-shore that provides excellent protection from high waves and rip currents. Like swimming in a lake that's full of sun worshippers and swimmers.

I came upon a tikki-bar with a palm frond roof and two guys with a covered table sitting by themselves. They looked way out of place. I made eye contact with the short one and he waved me over. He tells me his name is James---not Jim---James! A little fussy about his name, especially after looking him over. His clothes haven't been washed in along time. Same with his teeth because they're all black and worn down with neglect. Hails from somewhere in the states where they have flat square faces with eyes a little too close together. He's a lot younger than his buddy Felix, from Stuttgart, Germany. Felix has a slim moustache and thinning brown hair, wrinkled up corduroy pants and cowboy boots. Tall with a muscular build; the peak of health compared to his drinking buddy James. All his belongings are in an old navy duffle bag by his chair. They tell me they're going to Africa. I called to the waiter to bring me a cerveza and sit down to hear their story. I just know it's going to be interesting.

Felix has already been to Africa and a whole lot of other places. He's about forty years old and has been traveling—that's running—since he was twenty-six. A few more beers pass and I ask him why he's been traveling so long. He said he had a two year old daughter and a date to marry her mother but got cold feet as the wedding approached.

He waited till the day before the wedding and took off, never to be heard from by them again. Ran right out of England and as far East as he could go. When he ran out of land in India he bought an old Chinese junk with two other guys—both German. They set sail for Indonesia.

When they hit bad weather off the coast of Burma the boat broke up and only two of them made it to shore. This was Burma now. The communists were in power and the system was hostile to foreigners and anyone else that looked disagreeable. His friend had a gold watch that he bought in India before they left and all the Burmese kept starring at it. Felix told him to take it off, but he wouldn't, too proud of it, said "It looked great." Must have,--- because it cost him his life.

Felix made it down to Jakarta, Indonesia and went to the US consulate. They were very interested in getting all the information he had on the situation in Burma. He worked out a deal to give up all his information for a five year visa for the US. They told him to leave his passport with them and they would have it for him tomorrow with the visa when he would give the information.

Next day Felix came for the de-briefing and asked if his passport was ready. The assistant to the consular asked if he had given the information. Felix said he had, so he picked up his passport with the visa and walked out.

I asked "Did you ever give them the information?"

"Hell no, let them get their own damn information."

I thought ---another brilliant move by my government.

So we are under the palm fronds on the beach looking out over the sun backed tourists drinking beer and living large when Felix starts revealing his plan. It's sounding good and I'm seriously thinking about going along.

Here's the way it went: We take a ship leaving in a couple of days from Las Palmas to Mauritania on the west coast of Africa---then South through Senegal, Gambia, and all along the Ivory Coast until we reach the Trans African Highway. From there it's South till we hit Cape Town. We can work in the diamond mines because they are always looking for 'good' help says Felix. The diamonds are literally lying on the ground or just beneath the surface. Anyone caught "in the fields" or when leaving mine property is searched.

I ask "Well how do you get the diamonds out?"

"You have to stick them somewhere no one will find them." He says.

"Hmmmm" I say. Are a few small ones as valuable as one large one?"

We all crack up.

"I'll go"---I say, making a well thought out decision.

Felix says we should bring some watches to trade for food, rides and lodging. Said the Africans love them. But they have to have a minute hand so they can see that they work. The ones that tick the loudest were most valuable for the same reason. You could have a Swiss made Rolex but no minute hand---no good. Buying them was going to be fun.

The watch merchants, you know---the one's you've seen in every tourist trap all over the world. They walk up to you and roll up their sleeve and there is an arm full of watches to pick from, or open their coat and there's a jewelry store inside. These are the guys we'll be dealing with—Oh boy, I can here it now. "For you my friend, a special price."

We had a lot of laughs while buying the watches. The vendors would be pointing out the better one's and we'd say "Nope, too quiet!" They'd suggest "Omega?" We'd say "Nope, no minute hand." We're banging them on the table and dipping them in our beer and the vendors are going nuts.

Felix takes a watch and starts banging it a little too hard and the crystal pops off and pieces fly out. I'm laughing so hard, I fall off my chair. Now this guy is really pissed off and starts yelling. He wants money for the broken one. Felix stands up, all six feet three of him, intimidates the guy and tells him to bugger off. He calls out to his fellow vendors for help. They take one look at Felix, James and me. It becomes painfully obvious to this guy---and us---"he's on his own." But the jig is up. No one's going to sell us any more watches. That's okay; we've got all we need. And----"At a special price!"

~~~~

Ship's departure was advancing. I needed a Malaria shot for Africa and had it set up at a public clinic in Las Palmas. I'd heard a story of somebody getting hepatitis from the clinic but it was half the price of the hospital-- so the clinic it was.

I found it at the edge of town. They show me in to see the doctor. He's tall and thin with white hair and a white, pencil thin mustache. Old but in good shape, reminds me of my Uncle PJ a little. He turns and asks me what I want? "I need the malaria shot to go to Muaritania."

He hesitates for a moment, then reaches for a jar full of some kind of yellow liquid and pulls out a syringe and a big needle. Much bigger than what he needs for this job I'm sure. Puts the syringe and needle together, picks up a vial of something and draws out some fluid, turns and walks toward me. I don't know if it's fear or what but I start blabbing to him about my father being a doctor and how he died when I was thirteen, my mother being a nurse and I'm on my way to Africa and South to the diamond mines blah blah blah.

He pushes the juice into my arm, pulls out the needle and starts to walk away. Then stops, turns around and comes back to me---takes his finger and pokes me in the center of my chest, looks me in the eye and says "Don't go!"

Time stops---he turns and walks out of the room. I'm stunned. I sit there for what feels like a long time trying to grasp what just happened. The room comes alive again when someone enters. I leave. I can't feel the stairs below my feet as I walk down. Two blocks down the road there's an outside bar where I get a beer and sit and ponder what just happened. Either it's the effects of the shot or there's a message here. I keep replaying the scene in the office time and time again "Don't go!—Don't go!"

I recall a story my father told me when I was a boy. He was in medical school and stayed out partying too late and spent more money than he realized. He was along way from home and didn't have enough money for the street car, it was freezing and he was 'in trouble.' A woman got off the street car counting her money when a gust of wind blew a dollar bill out of her hand and down the street. My dad ran it down and brought it back to the woman but she was nowhere to be found,---but he had his fare to get home. I believe this is one of those stories.

Don't go!" I get it! I fight it because it's not what I want to do—but I get it. I'm not going to Africa. Not now. I did later, but not now.

I met Felix and James later that day. Told them the story and that I wasn't going with them. I don't think James got it. Felix was skeptical. Both of them put me through the wringer for changing my mind, calling me a weak whoosie with no backbone. Hell, they made me think of that yankee that wouldn't go to Europe with me as he had promised. I still think he was a whoosie. To me---my story was almost tangible. But it doesn't really matter. Though some things remain a mystery--- this was quite clear.

The boat to Mauritania was leaving the next night. She was a small ship, smaller than the passenger ship I came down on from Spain. We had a last beer together and I wished them good luck. Broke my bottle on the bow as I left; the sailor on watch yelled something at me, I raised both arms in a gesture of 'Hey—so what!' and walked back into town.

~~~

I never saw those guys again. Before we split up, Felix gave me a letter to give to his parents in Stuttgart if I ever got there. I told him I would –and I did. About a year later I was passing through and looked them up. Gave them the letter from Felix and they invited me to spend the night. They asked repeated questions about him—most of which I couldn't answer.

The next morning they gave me a letter to give to him should we ever meet again. It was a sad time. I thought of my mother. I carried that letter for three years and finally opened it because it was fraying so badly. It was very sad. Felix, if you're reading this—call home.

15. North Bound

To see Europe was my original plan, not sub Sahara Africa or Black Africa as its known. Now that I'd made that decision and was acting on it, I felt a lot better. It was the beginning of March and spring would be breaking out up North soon. But the travelers I met heading South said it was still pretty cold, in fact, one of the coldest winters on record.

I bought a 4th class ticket for the boat back to Cadiz, like I did on the way down with the hope of moving up to 2nd class after leaving port. Worked fine before but this time I ran into a problem.

It was the same shipping company and same type of ship. I thought it only had three decks but I was to find out there was a fourth. When I came aboard the steward looked at my ticket and pointed toward the bow. The next steward pointed down a stairwell below deck that at least had some port holes. Not bad I thought, until the next guy points down another set of stairs into what I thought was the engine room or bilge. There was no light and no air---I could hear that familiar groaning moaning sound I knew so well from previous voyages—and hell—we hadn't even left the dock yet!

I went down a few steps to where I could just make out what looked to be about three hundred Spanish paratroopers who had just finished their tour of duty fighting in the Spanish Sahara. A track of sand between Morocco and Mauritania—they'd been fighting over for years. I made a quick assessment—face the paratroopers in the stinking bilge—or the pushy steward on deck. I chose the steward!! I jumped up those few steps and got right into his face and pointed up to the next deck and said "Second class!" He pointed down! I inched forward, nose to nose, and gave him my most vile and crazy look-- pointed up and yelled "Second class." I don't know if my spit hit him in the eye---or his fear, but he blinked first—I had him. I grabbed my bag and headed up to second class, found an empty bunk and threw my stuff on it. Even if I had to pay the 2nd class fare at least I'd survive the trip. Down below with the paratroopers---I had my doubts.

   I laid low for a day before coming out. Nobody from the ship ever challenged me or asked for my ticket. Yes, it was another example of my 'goodwill ambassadorship.' Spreading peace, love and understanding on behalf of my country!!

~~~~

   Karl, or Kalley, to his friends, was from Hamburg. Tall and thin with dishwater blond hair and a moustache to match. He couldn't understand why I didn't speak German—what—was I stupid? I think it was because he was a little shy with his English. You know, worried someone would laugh if he made some grammatical mistake. Hell, I'd been laughed at so often at school by the East Coasties---I had an in-depth understanding. Anybody that laughs at you while you're trying to speak their language is an arrogant slob. The point is communication! Reminds me of the guy that asked "What do you call a guy that speaks three languages?" -----Trilingual. "How about a guy that speaks two languages?"-----Bilingual. "How about one language?"----Yep—American!

I met Kalley on the fan-tail of the ship blowing huge smoke rings out to sea from a chillum full of hashish and tobacco. He handed me the chillum and try as though I did-- just couldn't get the hang of the smoke rings. Didn't affect the buzz though! Told me he was an electrician in Hamburg and on a two week holiday for some fun and sun in the Canaries. Said he had four more weeks.

"What?" I asked

"Ya, I have six weeks of holidays each year and take them two weeks at a time so it's not so long between them," He says.

I'm thinking 'Is this the devastating socialism I've been warned about all my life?'

I said "In the States after one year you get two weeks and after fifteen or twenty years you get three weeks and certainly no more than four. Then the company starts looking for a younger guy to take your job and pay them less.

He just laughed. I didn't think it was funny. Part of my education!

A Canadian guy came up to us and introduced himself to me as Frank. Him and Kalley had met in the Canaries and were heading North together. Kalley for home; Frank was going to Paris to improve his French. Seems the French they speak in Canada wasn't quite the same.

Frank was about 5'10" with red hair and fair complexion, he had a few freckles from the sun like I get. He was wearing a light weight full length leather coat of good quality and a shirt with a real collar, pants—not jeans. He was an artist.

Said he was twenty-seven and a student at McGill University in Montreal.
I asked with a questioning look on my face, "Twenty-Seven-- eh Frank? And a student?"

"Well I've changed my major a few times;--You might call me a professional student."

I laughed and said "Yeah, we've got a lot of those back in the States with the war and all." Yet I knew I'd have to face that when I went back home.

Frank says "He wants to be called Angelo, it's his middle name."

I asked "Why he introduced himself as Frank?"

Everybody wants a new identity when they travel. Something more exciting than their hum-drum, stayed or boring—real name---they think.

I said, "You made the Freudian slip Frank. It's burned into my brain and I doubt if I can change now."
Pissed him off a bit. But hey!

We toked up and looked over the rail into the prop wash from the ship. Watching the gulls dive down into that froth and pull something out, time and again. How can they see anything in that? It's all in the eye!

~~~~

Those guys had plans and destinations. I was just heading North---with neither.

When the boat docked and we had to get to the train station, Frank saw some advantage to my poor Spanish. And poor it was. Kind of reminded me of a dog walking on its hind legs.—It doesn't do it very well,--but it's a wonder it does it at all.

I did get us through every train change and from station to station through Madrid and up to Barcelona and into France where Frank and his "French" took over. I think everybody was impressed.

   It was going to be a long train ride across Spain. I had a nice piece of hash and so did Kalley. We bought a bottle of Pernod and with a few tokes, the trip was turning into fun. We'd be talking about something and Frank would make a quick sketch about it and we'd laugh and laugh about something the next day couldn't work up even a smile. I love it.

   I think Frank's impression of me was that of a poorly educated, naïve Midwestern boy and he probably wasn't far off the mark. Course you need to take into consideration that inferiority---love/hate screen most Canadians see us Americans through.

   Frank was twenty-seven and had a couple of degrees. I was eighteen and had one semester of college. But I saw and experienced more in my first month in Europe than my whole life in St. Louis. Especially concerning the interesting people and places I visited.

   Why hell, if Rapunzel would have been home when Jeff called to her in Luxemburg,--I would have climbed that tower and might still be there. So it's one month down and five more to go. I'm catching on and catching up. Drinking it in and soaking it up like a sponge---and loving every minute.

~~~

   We stayed in Barcelona for a couple of days and went back to the little restaurant that served great paella and wine. The small plaza had a church whose bells peeled off on the quarter hour. On one corner was a rotisserie that was built into the wall with a half dozen chickens slowly turning a golden brown. We had one of those before the night was through. Delicious!!

The sights and smells of the cafés, restaurants and bars was intoxicating---or maybe it was the wine? We made our way back to the pension "Clave" [The Key} where I'd stayed before. The huge door was still impressive. When I knocked, the old lady—Rosita—still in black, answered and was genuinely happy to see me—and I her. Since there were three of us she showed us a bigger room with its own toilet. 'Moving on up.'

The shower was down the hall—no hot water. That made me miss the ship a little.

I still had about four grams of hash wrapped in tin foil. I didn't want to carry it and nobody else did because of the stories we'd heard of people getting picked up—searched and thrown in jail.

In the bathroom was a light fixture on a steel tube—same low wattage bulb, but this one had a lantern type glass surround. It looked to be the perfect place to hide the shit. That's what everyone called hashish—shit. So we toked up before we left and I stuck the shit in the light fixture. When the light was on you could just barely see it---didn't throw much light anyway.

Off we went into the city. A few hours later we came back and I checked the hash. It was gone!! Rosita must have found it. Now the paranoia starts. Rosita has our passports as well. That's the law. You have to give up your passport whenever you check into a hotel—all over Europe. So there's no taking off! Paranoia's getting a stronger grip. What now? We start looking around. Under the bed, in the corners, the floor, the waist basket, and then I look in the toilet. There it is--still in the foil—sitting on the dry side of the bowl. I call Frank and Kalley over and point to it and say

"Hey man, the shits in the toilet!!"
With a sigh of relief Frank says "Well of course it is. Where else would the shit be but in the toilet!"
Then Kalley pipes in—the same thing in German and we all crack up. We laugh and laugh---off and on for hours. Even years latter when we would meet we'd laugh about it.

Rosita must have been cleaning—found the tinfoil in the light—and thrown it into the toilet. What a cleaner, and what a relief for us! Franco's Spain instilled fear in everyone.

16. St. Louis Flashback

We went out to breakfast at a café on the Ramblas. Frank was in the lead and sat down where the tables had tablecloths---always the upscale guy. He had complained about the pension a little—not the price mind you—just the accommodations. Nice to have your cake and eat it too. The sun was up and warm as we sat down. Felt great since the room where we were staying had no windows and would cool down considerably by morning. Café con leche and a croissant were the standard fair. The French croissants were lighter and more flakey—but that's not to say the Spanish ones were bad.

I was sitting back and soaking up the heat and waiting for the caffeine to kick in when Kalley starts getting excited. He's reading a German newspaper from Hamburg and is pointing to an article telling of a pop-festival that's going to start in 10 days. Kalley's more animated than I've ever seen him before. He's usually more quiet and reserved, but not now. He's going on and on in German until Frank grabs his arm and says "Hey---Hey—English man." Kalley catches on and explains; it's a three day pop-festival with a bunch of big name bands. We should all go together. He can find us a place to stay and we'd have a blast. I look over at Frank. He shrugs and says "My French and Paris can wait." I've got visions of Woodstock rolling around in my mind. So I say "It's a no-brainer for me, let's go!

Kalley wanted to get going back to Hamburg. Something about seeing his girl friend before going back to work and letting her know about Frank and I coming along. He got his stuff together and we walked him to the train station to say good bye and to check the schedule for the trains North. Our best bet was to take the express, leaving in the morning. We figured to ride through France and Switzerland into Germany, then get out and hitch-hike. That left us one more night in Barcelona.

Frank went to a Salvatore Dalli museum. I took a walk around town down by the port not far from our pension in the lower echelon of the city. Getting thirsty—I ducked into a dive with sawdust and cast-offs on the floor. The smell of smoke, stale beer and spilled wine permeated the air---until ya got to the bar where the sausages and hams hanging from the ceiling took over. I love these places. A glass of wine for a nickel. Damn!

Once my eyes adjusted from the bright sun outside to the dark caver-ness inside I noticed a light-skinned black guy with a leather hat and leather vest, jeans and boots on, leaning against the bar drinking wine and talking with a couple of locals. We made eye contact as I ordered a glass of wine and we exchanged a few words. He was obviously American—probably he thought the same of me.

"Where you from?" I ask.

"St. Louis." He says

"Bullshit."

"No man, really—I'm from St. Louis." He says.

"Nobody's from St. Louis." I say. "At least nobody I met since taking off."

"Well, I am." He states.

"Where abouts" I ask.

"Webster Groves" He says. My jaw must have hit the bar. He's stunned at my response

"Me too" I say "Born and raised there. It's a great place----to be away from"
He tells me his name is Tommy. He's not from Webster but his dad has a car dealership there and he's traveling through Europe for a few months.

"Name's George and I'm traveling around as well, but should be back before the fall semester starts in September. This calls for a celebration." I buy a bottle of Champaign and Tommy and I walk outside and sit on the dock overlooking the harbor where we can talk without distraction. I crack open the Champaign and start toasting St.Louis—Webster Groves—and whatever else comes to mind. We went through the first bottle pretty quick, Tommy bought the second. We were fast-friends now, swapping stories—past and present, some lies and some dreams for the future.

I tell him I'm going to Hamburg for a pop-festival and ask if he wants to come along?
He says he's heading North as well—to Paris, but sticking around here for a few more days. But maybe we'd see each other again.

We did---twice. It was in Paris, at the "Café du Monde." I was having a café and cognac. They say if you sit at the Café du Monde long enough you will see the whole world pass by. Because everyone will pass by the Café du Monde at sometime in their life. I know there are poems, plays and movies with that theme---so it must be true---no?

I was looking down at a newspaper—missing the passing world—when Tommy approaches me on my blind side, casually touches my arm and says "Hello George."

I look up; see him and flip out. Jump up and greet him loudly saying, "Hey Tommy, what's happening? Good to see you man. Where you been?" Blah blah blah. Meanwhile, Tommy's acting cool and calm. The people around us are looking at me like I'm goofy. Trouble is---they're right. But if that's the last time I look goofy I'll be happy.

Tommy's laughing. Now I get it.

A couple months later, Tommy's in a Chinese restaurant in Amsterdam with two good looking blonds. I see him through the window but he doesn't see me. I approach him on his blind side and say "Hello Tommy" and it's his turn to jump up and act the fool. I just smile. He gets it. We look at each other and know it probably won't happen again. I looked him up back in St.Louis. He was plugged back into the system working for his dad at the car dealership, living that bourgeois lifestyle we all wanted to avoid.

The sun was long gone but Tommy and I were still sitting on the dock talking and drinking. We finished the second bottle of Champaign and I stood up and threw it as hard as I could at a passing freighter. Not even close. But it seemed to be the appropriate gesture at the time. In the early 70's the harbors were filled with crap.—They're better now.

We went back into the bar and carried on. I stumbled back to my pension in the wee hours of the morning. Of course it's locked. I start yelling for Rosita to open the door. There's no response. I yell louder. A window opens and a guy sticks his head out and says something I can't understand but starts clapping his hands. What the f___. I don't want any applause—I want the damn door opened. I yelled again. No response. Rosita must be sleeping in the bedroom farthest away from the street, I think. My answer, yell louder. A passer-by stopped and told me to clap my hands. Son of a b___! I know I'm loaded but what the hell is clapping my hands going to do? But I start. Clap Clap Clap.

Lo and behold! A guy in a tattered old uniform with a bus drivers' hat comes walking around the corner. I swear he looks just like Josef Stalin minus the boots. He reaches deep into his coat pocket and comes up with a set of huge keys. Picks one out, sticks it into the lock on my door, turns it and opens the door. Gestures for me to enter and holds out his hand discretely. I gave him the equivalent of a dollar, trying to buy off my obvious stupidity. He's ecstatic and I'm in my pension. All part of the education!!

17. Deutschland!

Time was creeping up on the weekend of the pop-festival in Hamburg. Frank and I took the train straight through to a small town in southern Germany called Tubingen, a university town-- which always means a lot of good bars and clubs.

There was a cool Island in the middle of the river--the Neckar River—and by the map I could tell it was upstream from Heidelberg which was on the list of places to see. There was also a 15th-century church of St. George whose architecture and age struck a deep chord in me. I had never seen anything so old yet such a solid and strong depiction of an eternal heritage. Being from St. Louis, if anything was fifty or sixty years old you tore it down—a hundred years old was ancient—tear that old crap down and build new!!! That was the right idea---no?

St. George was the "Dragon Slayer" well known throughout Europe and England. I'd never heard of him and yet history was always a favorite course. I wondered how I missed that—Why--- I had the best education in the world—or so I was told.

We went to the youth hostel. No cheap pensions in Germany. No sawdust on the floors in the bars either. We were back in the heart of civilization. Ahh--but the food and drink were good.

"Jugendherbere" means youth hostel in German. When spoken properly and if the person speaking is standing directly in front of you, it will always in-tale a small bit of saliva hitting you in the eye as they speak. So when asking directions---duck.

They locked us in early--exactly 10:00 PM, at 10:30---lights out. Morning started much too early! Military marching music was blaring loudly over the loud speakers at 6:00AM. I hit my head on the guys bunk above me and wondered, if I got so screwed-up last night that I joined the "Hitler Jugend."

Frank got up and did a loud "Sieg Heil." I cracked up---nobody else was laughing! Everybody got up and marched to the dining hall for breakfast where all things were lined up in their proper place. Coffee, tea, brotchens, cheese, bread, jam and various cold cuts—a fantastic breakfast. This was my first and last youth hostel in Germany.

~~~~

It's still cold up North. We head out on the road dressed in winter clothes. Frank's got a nice coat—I'm layered up. After about half an hour I start sinking. Hitch-hiking is supposed to be good in Germany. A big German guy walks up to try his luck as well. He's got a big leather coat and hat on and looks warm as toast. I'm freezing my ass off. He asks us "How its going?"

"We're still here!" I said.

"Where are you going?" He asks.

"Hamburg" Frank answers.

"You need to have a sign so people know where you want to go." He says as he tears his card board sign in half and gives us a piece. "Now, write ha ha on it for Hamburg."

"What?!"

"Ja, write ha ha on your sign."

Frank and I look at each other and start laughing.
I say "Damn Frank,---with all that education and you didn't know to write ha ha on our sign?" We go back and forth on that for a minute. Then the guy explains how each major city in Germany has one or two letters that appear first on the license plate to indicate which city the car is from.
He's telling us ha ha are the letters H H in the German alphabet indicating Hamburg.
Frank thought that was a good idea. I thought it was about control.

We wrote H H for Hamburg on our sign and still waited. I'd done some hitch-hiking in the States---especially in my junior year of high school in 1968. I figured Hamburg was too far from southern Germany, so I flipped our sign over and wrote a big "F" on it.

"Ya got a few of these in school, didn't ya Frank?" I said.

It didn't take long before we had a ride to Frankfort. From there, we were on the main Autobahn running North and South. We had good luck all the way up to the outskirts of Hamburg. Didn't wait long when a beat-up, faded green VW bug pulled up.

Volker [Fall-ka] was driving. He was eighteen years old---not even a year younger than me. Six feet five inches tall, thick black hair that looked like he cut it himself without a mirror, lean and strong.

Volker was a deep thinker as well. From his low resonating voice came some of the most profound things I'd ever heard. This from a guy my age---speaking in a second language---using a few words that were not yet in my vocabulary. We were discussing some engineering problem and he came up with a math concept that impressed me.

"Where did you learn that?" I asked.

"My father taught me that when I was a child." Hmmm, interesting I thought.

The three of us, Frank, Volker and I became friends for years. But Volker came to a very sad ending.

We met him on the autobahn just South of Hamburg. He was returning from his home town of Heidelberg to start his first year of art school. The beat-up old volks already had two hitch-hikers and their gear inside. Fred and I pushed and shoved our stuff in, finally making room for all five of us. Reminded me of the times we'd seen how many people we could fit in a VW. This time it was just fine because body heat was about all we were feeling. The car had no heater.

Volker dropped the two students off at their stop and asked us where ours was. We said we had none but knew Kalley and he had a place for us. Since it was getting late Volker asked us if we wanted to stay with him. Said he had a studio. I don't know if that was accurate.

We drove up and parked on the sidewalk in front of a commercial building. Opened a side door and climbed a flight of stairs that opened into a huge room about fifty feet long and twenty-five feet wide. There were windows all along the wall facing the street and a wood plank floor.

The furnishings consisted of a table with one chair and a sleeping bag on a mattress on the floor. The room was located above a three bay garage that was closed, which meant no heat was radiating up from there. A beautiful old coal stove with delft blue tiles on the side and chrome trim was sitting in the middle of the room. I walked over, opened the door and said "Let's fire this thing up." Volker grumbles a little, from which I understood "There's no coal."

I think to myself "My new friend is living on a meager allowance."

It was as cold in there as it was outside, maybe colder. I went back outside and started scouring the alley ways and behind buildings looking for pallets or crates or something that would burn. Nothing, seems the Germans don't leave crap laying around in their alleys. Went back upstairs walked over and looked into the stove again. There was at least three inches of firebrick as a liner in the stove. I knew it would take hours to get it hot and even then I doubt the room would get warm. We rolled out our sleeping bags on that cold floor and went to sleep. Not an easy task. It was from Volker that I learned how to take a deep breath and shout "schiess kalt!" Believe me it was shit cold!

18. The Popfestival

The Pop Festival started the next night. We all three went and had a great time. Met Kalley inside with some of his friends and got a warm welcome with a big chillum of hash and tobacco, the first of many. Good music, big smoke and wild times for three days straight. I remember going in and the first group, Black Sabbath. After that it's a bit of a blur.

When the music stopped, Frank and I went with Volker back to his place. It wasn't any warmer.

Kalley had a place for us with some friends of his who rented out the basement of a mansion in a well to do part of the city. The house was old and huge. The cellar had big concrete and stone arches holding up the main structure. This made for a big room in the center of the cellar with about a dozen rooms opening onto it. Each room was rented by someone and most every night there wood be music and partying in the center room.

The owner was a big dealer. Very big. The police didn't really bother the little dealers but they sure looked hard on the big ones. They wanted the owner of this house. They made a raid one evening and tore up the big house upstairs looking for the hash, but couldn't find it. The next day the owner was laughing and joking how stupid the police were because they didn't look into the pantry with a false wall. The cops showed up at that same moment and found five hundred kilos of hash. I met that guy one time. After that I never saw him again.

Down stairs in the cellar was a different scene. Good times, fun and partying with good people. Half the rooms were rented by guys in a band that was trying to make it big. One room was rented by Jorgen. A small framed guy--- skinny as a rail with stringy brown hair and a bad complexion. He was a heroin addict. Heck of a nice guy to me but everyone else warned me not to trust him. He kept offering to let me use his works [needle and syringe] but I continually declined. He was the first heroin addict I got to know.

~~~~

It took awhile to warm up to Kalley's friends. Things were going real well with Volker so we stuck together. The pop festival was the start of the party. We kept it going and didn't see the sun for another three weeks, except at dawn or dusk.

One of the things Volker showed us was the night life and another was how the Germans drive. One was as interesting as the other. The Germans know one way to drive---flat out---pedal to the metal. It was that way on the autobahn always, but Volker drove that way in the city too. With every gear change the accelerator slams back to the floor.

The lights don't go from red to green in Germany. The yellow light goes on while the red is still on. This means to rev up your engine and put it in gear causes it's going to turn green and when it does, the race is on. If you're in the crosswalk and you hear the gears grinding and the engines revving up you better get your ass to the side walk fast because if you're out there when the light turns green, you're fair game. And if you're out of the crosswalk or jay-walking at any time, it's open season on you. I don't care if you're a ninety year old woman on crutches.

It's intimidating as hell crossing the street. The light starts to change; you hear the motors and look at the driver you're walking in-front of. He looks at you, then the light, then back at you and smiles. You can see he's hoping you won't make it so he can kill you and get by with it.

We drove like that all the time. Racing-down the streets, parking on the sidewalks and not once were we pulled over. I saw the cops look at us a couple of times but they never stopped us. You couldn't smoke, drink or eat because it was too rough a ride.

~~~

We got to know the Hamburg nightlife. The clubs, bars and of course the Reeperbahn. It's a wonder I made it through all that. You'll see why--- later. The Reeperbahn was notorious to anyone with any knowledge of Hamburg and world renowned for its legal prostitution. Located a few blocks up from the port where roaming seamen would leave their semen in some willing prostitute, having a wild time while they did.   All this---under the watchful eye of the tower of the church of St. Michaels.

~~~

Climbing up from the U-bahn station [subway] to the main street was a hard pull. Reeperbahn---one long row of clubs, bars, restaurants, dance-halls and all manor of bazaar shops where one could buy what ever tickled one's sexual fantasies. The further down the street you went, the seedier it got. Until you arrive at the "Eros center" where the whores are haggling over their wares and who knows for sure whether they're male or female.

Stepping off onto a side street behind the metal partition is where the higher priced prostitutes can be found, sitting behind a glass window on view to all. Like a sweet-cake, one prettier than the next and all government inspected! But why buy what you can have for free?

There is the Sahara Club, run by the Persians. The Brun Halle, run by the Germans. Both hate each other and war over the drug trade. I like the Sahara because the music is better and there seems to be more unattached, beautiful girls. That's where I met Anka. I came in and cruised the place to see what was up and then went straight to the dance floor. If you sit down some one tries to sell you an expensive drink.

There she was, on the dance floor, dancing with a girlfriend. I danced over and got in between them and said "Hey"

She responded with "My name is Anka."

I was obviously a foreigner which sparked her interest. She wanted to try the English she's been learning since fifth grade. I'm willing. She has blue eyes and dishwater blonde hair, some past her shoulders and the rest chopped off in layers up to her ears. That rebellious look I find so attractive.

"That's for me" I think. With almost no make-up on she's going to look the same tomorrow morning as she does now. A natural beauty. I'm falling fast.

We make small talk.

"I'm American, from St.Louis, Missouri"

"I know, I can tell by your accent." She says. Hers is English.
Her friend leaves to sit down and it's just her and me. Great!

"I'm here on a holiday for a few months. I've only been in Hamburg for five days. I came for the pop-festival"
She gives me a wary eye and says "You smoke shit?"

"Sure" I say, and drink beer." Thinking that should be a plus.

"I don't do either one." She says with a strong accent on the 'I'.

"Then you're not German. There's more beer drunk here per capita than anywhere in the world."

"You need to get out of the bars George." She says and smiles.
I lean close and say "Let's get out of this one."

We walk out of the Sahara Club, into the crisp night air on our way to the U-bahn station to take the train to her place. "Life is good and getting better."

~~~

We stayed together in her place for a few days, where we shared each others passions and desires and brought each others bodies to that convulsing ecstasy of joy and fulfillment that can only be experienced fully by those who are free and unencumbered.
And to those American men who retract from a few hairs under the arms of a beautiful girl---or are repulsed from those blonde hairs on their legs I say "Stay home. I'll take care of it from here."

~~~

The Germans who wanted to control the drug scene were constantly at war with the Persians. All those beautiful Persian carpets in the show room windows that you admire were at one time rolled up full of kilos of hashish or raw opium inside and shipped from Iran. The Persians would sell the dope and start a legitimate business with the proceeds. That was common knowledge on the street, everybody knew about it except the German customs officials.

I liked the Sahara Club. Anka and I met there and I wanted to go back together again the next night. Anka had other plans and was adamant we do what she wanted to do. Hey---I'm easy. The next day she came up with the newspaper and showed me the front page. "Seven people killed in the Sahara Club on the Reeperbahn" by a German rival gang. Seems a bunch of Germans came into the club and started shooting---killing four Persians and three tourists. That could have been us, I thought. 'Hmmm---- maybe another divine hand in my life.' I must say I was glad to have been with Anka that night.

Within the week the Persians got their revenge. Loaded up with machine pistols (German made fully-automatic pistols) and clubs, the Persians shot their way into a German club killing another half dozen people. All this over the drug trade and talk was that it would get worse.

~~~

The fire and passion between Anka and I burned out about as fast as it was kindled. And after the killings at the night clubs, I figured it was a good time to see Amsterdam.

Looking back, it was a great experience to visit the Reeperbahn and the "Eros center," seeing the whores, prostitutes and all manor of bazaar behavior on the late night scene in the city. It was 'live circus' and when in Hamburg, one must see the circus. It's a little different on each visit. And you'll always take away something to remember.

One night I saw a bouncer in front of a strip joint get into a fight with a smaller guy. The bouncer was huge---looked like a wrestler. The kind I'd seen eating whole chickens with a plate full of potatoes and sauerkraut and washing that down with two liters of beer. He wasn't wearing a hat because I doubt if he could find one that fit.

Maybe the other guy wasn't so small, as he was dwarfed, by the size of the bouncer. Another bystander told me the smaller guy was a black belt in karate. Mr. 'karate' started waving his arms around and chopping the air and getting into the 'spirit.' Then jumped in and hit the bouncer five times in quick succession. Three times in the face and two times in the solar plexus, steps back, jumps into the air and kicks the 'moose' in the head. Just like in the movies. Only the bouncer hasn't moved an inch. Mind you his head sure jerked back when he got kicked. But then he smiled---smiled, and set about tying Mr. 'karate' in a knot. There's never a dull moment at the circus.

19. The SS Officer

The fun was done with Anka. I was back with Frank and Volker, sleeping on the frozen floor at Volkers place. It must have been a record winter because it was cold all the time. Cold waiting for the U-bahn, cold walking the streets, cold on the floor of most of the bars,---and when your feet are cold----you're cold. Cold! Cold! Cold!

We took to drinking grogs. A healthy shot of cognac in a glass of hot water with a couple of cubes of sugar and a twist of lemon. After the first one, you're warming up. After the second, it's "Hey, what did we come in here for?"

Check this out: Frank, Volker and I are sitting at the bar working on our third when a guy at a table calls us over. I noticed him earlier watching us and trying to listen in on our conversation. He's a carpenter. You can tell by his heavy corduroy 'zimmermans hosen'---pants, with double zippers in the front and a double breasted vest and matching hat. He has a medium build with close cropped brown hair and piercing green eyes. I figure him to be between fifty to fifty-five years old. Which was odd in itself seeing how there's so few men that age in Germany. Much older or younger---yes, but the majority of men his age are dead from the war. He speaks English pretty well and tells us he lived in Canada and the US. We talk on for awhile and then he says "My place isn't far from here and it's nice and warm." Magic words to me!

Looking at Frank and me, he says "I have good German food I can heat up. You buy a bottle of cognac and bring it along for after."

We look at each other, shrug and say "Why not?"

"Hell, he had me at "warm" I say

It's easy enough to get a bottle of cognac on the street with all the mom and pop shops. His place is only a couple of blocks away and he meets us at the door.

Sure enough, it's on the fourth floor and all the heat from the flats below is radiating up and the floor is warm. He works in the kitchen for awhile and comes out with four plates full of pork, potatoes and sauerkraut. It's delicious! We all help clear the table and then set about drinking the cognac.

One drink, two drinks and the tongue loosens and the stories begin to flow. He tells us he left Germany just after the armistice and went to Canada where he worked as a lumberjack, cutting down and hauling trees out of the bush. Says he worked his way across the country and when he got to British Columbia decided to go south into the States. He loved Washington and Oregon and continued down into northern California.   The Korean War was in full swing and every eligible man had to register. They were drafting everybody they could. He told them he had been in the German army and was tired of war. They answered, since he had experience he would likely be drafted.
I asked "You really think the Americans would have drafted you?"

"Hell yes" he says "They were taking everybody.

"Yeah, they're doing that now, for Vietnam." I say.

He says "I had to take a physical. The doctor and an officer were questioning me about my German army experience and when they found out I was an officer in the SS-----------He stops, he knows he screwed-up---there's dead silence in the room except for a passing car in the street. He looks at us and says "But I had nothing to do with the Jews!

"Yeah, right!"----Nobody did!" I say.

Damn, did I drink so much I'm having a re-run of the Nuremburg trials in my brain?
Maybe it's a flashback from the acid I took at the pop-festival. No--- this is happening.

From this point on the congeniality of the situation starts deteriorating. He starts telling us about the fire-bombings that Hamburg went through. How the streets would be filled with fire up to the third and fourth floors. If the fire was in the front of the building the people would run to the back to get air. If the fire was in the front and back they died because the fire sucked all the oxygen out of the air. War is hell for everyone. But was he telling me this as some accounting for his actions in the war? His statement about the Jews was still almost tangible in the room.

My brain spaces out thinking about what we've been talking about but I'm thrust back into reality when I hear him say something about "only following orders."
By this time my rebellious spirit is well lubricated and I say "These orders, yes sir no sir, it's all a lot of bullshit."

Now Frank and I are both leaning back in our chairs, while Volker is sitting upright and watching.

The old SS officer leans forward and slams his hand down on the table hard enough to make all the drinks jump up an inch and stand at attention, then yells "Nine!--- this is the backbone of the fatherland."

I fall forward to upright in my chair. Frank falls over backwards in his. Volker is stunned and there's an awkward silence while Frank tries to recover himself from the floor. I start laughing because of Frank. Then all three of us crack up. We're all shit faced drunk. I look over at the old Nazi, his eyes are bulging out and he's not laughing. He's out of his chair, knees bent and standing on the balls of his feet looking like he's ready to spring into action. I think he thinks we're laughing at him. I try to cool him down but there's no use. He's hot. I know our visit is done. Sure enough he flips out and throws us all out into the street. It's three o'clock in the morning. Damn, back to Volkers ice cold studio.

Frank and I try to engage Volker in conversation about the war. What his parents went through or any stories he knew of, but he would have no part in it. He just grumbled something about being bad for everybody and that was it.

20. Hamburgers

Volker was attending art classes----sometimes. Frank left for Paris to perfect his French. Ya know there's only one place in the world where they speak true French? Yeah, you got it.

Volker had turned me on to a number of local pubs in the university district. All laid- back and local with lots of students and some new graduates trying to make their way in the world. Some with big dreams, needing just a little liquid courage to finalize and enact their plans.

Carpenters, electricians, plumbers and the everyday citizenry from their corner of the city, in their local pub.

King Soloman said "There is nothing better than for a man to eat and drink and enjoy the fruits of his labor." What wisdom!! I couldn't agree more. Smoking hashish was verboten however. One had to step outside and use some discretion---except in one establishment. Pretty well the same as the others except it was run by an old biker named charley. He must be about sixty with grey hair over his ears, the typical German beer gut and always wearing a t-shirt. Even in winter.

Charley was tough. Bikers or 'gamlers,' as the German's called this rougher element, and dealers frequented Charley's place, as did I, whenever I was in Hamburg. It was local and full of color. But within three years Charley would be stabbed to death and-----well, that's for later and another story.

~~~

Fritz was a friend of Volkers. He had curly brown hair, a thin face with a small over-bite, and his slightly crooked teeth matched up with his eyes because one was always looking to the left. And still he gave off an air of intelligence. His small framed silver granny glasses helped justify his good business sense. Starting out with part interest in a pub near the university and then ending up with a place of his own just a few doors down, which we frequented often.

Every town of any size in Germany had their own brewery and the locals were very proud of their regional product; bordering on a civic duty, and with good reason--- rarely was there a beer I didn't like.

There was no refrigeration for draft beer in the pubs in the early 70's. The beer was 'kellar warm' meaning it was as cold as the cellar the keg was in. Many believe the taste was enhanced this way instead of hiding behind a 'cold chill'. I just drank it, one after the other.

Fritz had to pump it up from the cellar and start filling glasses setting one aside and grabbing another as the foam hit the top of the glass. As the foam settled, he'd grab the glass again filling it up and repeating the process until the glass was full. Well worth waiting for, and delicious!

In one corner of his pub was a fussball game that never quit. Lots of local conversation and decent food, just a great place to meet people. Good vibes. It was here that I learned the proper etiquette of setting one's beer glass or mug on the table or bar after a healthy swig.

It goes as follows: first, never set your glass down as you would in the States, gently, so to speak. Doing so gives others the impression you're effeminate, weak in character or impotent; deficiencies that will certainly be noticed by the strong and manly.

The German method is to negotiate one's glass so that it's over the table or bar at any given height. The higher, the more intoxicated. Let gravity take over, dropping arm and glass simultaneously hitting the bar top, letting go of the glass immediately and let your hand slide off the bar and come to a rest either in your lap or arm of the chair---in one flowing motion. In Germany you are simply one of many. In the rest of the world you will have the attention of those around you and more importantly the bar tender, at which time you have the opportunity to order another beer.

21. The University

The world famous University of Hamburg is one of the elite institutions of learning in the world, full of people from every country, culture, ethnicity and background. Where enlightenment and knowledge are broken into a spectrum of variations, then further studied and explored and brought forth in some resplendent truth for our era. Only to be done again by next years class.

Here was the beauty of youth, the desire to learn and explore, to experience and test those things one has learned from their youth, whether they be true or not. An atmosphere I could have thrived on, if only I could have fully taken part. But I had no real residence, no residency papers and no money for classes.

I never experienced anything like this at my liberal arts college in Kansas City Missouri, where the East Coasties so rudely ruled.

At most every hour of the day, especially in the evening hours after dinner in the 'mensa' or student union, discussions were taking place on topics of a wide variety. I discovered this by frequenting the cafeteria for the cheap and plentiful food. Another bonus was so many smart beautiful girls who wanted to try out their English.

It was the discussions that drew my interest. They gave me a chance to develop and enlighten my own intellect.

With the war in Vietnam tearing at the social fabric back home, I gravitated toward the political. The most influential and domineering were the communists which broke down into their sub groups of Marxists, Leninists, Maoists and Trotskyites.

There were socialists, anarchists and fascists, although they were taboo, and even a few that were spouting the virtues of democracy. It did not escape me that our free and open discussions might not be possible in most of these systems. I can't imagine them taking place in Moscow or East Berlin.

Most people sat and listened, some with interest and some with indifference. Those 'leaders' most certain and authoritative in their beliefs who had the quick response to any question or objection I discovered, were not students at all, but 'party' members or political affiliates that were there on a daily basis. It was in effect, a recruiting ground.

We young and naive, with heads full of mush and the forceps scars barely faded were being molded into the beliefs of some 'new world order'. Doubtful the one your parents sent you here to learn about and certainly not to join. These guys were very convincing and well schooled in the art of persuasion.

I listened intently to all sides. When I went back to school the next semester I could regurgitate many of these beliefs and won most of the arguments. Because if you don't know your own system, how can you defend it? Like discussing religion without having read the Bible, or entering the "Tour de France' on a tricycle. You don't have a chance.

Two of these politico's were "Red Army". The same bunch that murdered an Italian prime minister and hung him from a bridge. Two others were in Beider/Meinhoff, a faction of Red Army named after James Beider and Ulrica

Meinhoff, two German anarchists operating robin-hood style with a gang; robbing the rich and helping the poor, but really mostly themselves. Yet they were very popular among the general population, especially the students.

    I kept running into one guy in particular, named Dieter Rink of Beider/Meinhoff, in different parts of the city. He was about five feet six inches tall. Small for German standards, which probably gave him that 'little guy' attitude. Pock-marked face and 'free-range' brown hair with inset eyes that moved side to side when he talked. It made him look like a squirrel watching for a hawk that might strike at any moment. We'd talk for awhile each time we met and after one such meeting he invited me over to meet some of his friends.

    This guy had 'fanatic' pasted all over him and I doubt if his 'friends' would be any different. I got stoned and missed the meeting. Glad I did. Beider ended up committing suicide in prison and Ulrica Meinhoff was shot dead while trying to shoot her way out of a bank robbery. In retrospect, I think Rink might have been trying to recruit me. "Why, oh why, did I miss that meeting?--------Thank you"

22. The Way to Amsterdam

"It's time to go to Amsterdam. This time I mean it."

The U-bahn took me to Wilhelmsburg and then the #115 bus to Kirchdorf. From there it was a matter of cutting through a couple of fields to get to a rest stop on the South bound Autobahn.

A great place to hitch-hike because the cars would stop for fuel, food, beer or whatever. Had to be great because there was twenty people ahead of me, all trying their luck. I started getting visions of Spain and France again. But it wasn't like that at all.

There were cars stopping all the time. We hitch-hikers spread out so there was about twenty feet between us. A car would stop and say where he was going and if the guy who was next in line wasn't going that way the next hitch-hiker took the ride.

It wasn't long before it was my turn. During my wait I must say, it was extremely thoughtful on the part of the German government to provide access to a variety of beers at the rest stop. The U.S could learn a few things here.

~~~

This is my ride pulling up now. A big black Mercedes Benz sedan with leather seats you melt into. The guy has a business suit and tie on and I ask him where he's going. To Essen---Yes? That's going to get me half the way to Amsterdam. We take off and he floors it. My first time ever in a big luxurious Mercedes Benz and I can't tell if it rides like a boat or a rocket---probably a combination of the two. The after burners kicked off at two hundred kilometers per hour [120 mph] and we cruise at that speed for awhile. The boat sensation kicks in and it feels like we're flying and floating.

The slow traffic, well, there's really no slow traffic. Everybody is going as fast as they can. There are only slow cars, and they are on the right side of the road. In fact, everybody drives on the right. After we fly by some guy we get back on the right and lo and behold we get passed doing 120 mph. Damn!

We come upon an accident where the ambulance is just leaving. Two cars collided and it looks like a pile of scrap metal. The ambulance is in no hurry and I ask the guy.

"Why isn't the ambulance speeding up?"

He looks at me like---yes, you're stupid, and says "At this speed nobody survives, so why hurry?"
I just nod in recognition because I'm a bit stunned.
We slow down for the accident but once past that we're back up to 120mph again.

I was always told "You don't get there any faster by speeding." Well, those people never road at 120 mph on a German Autobahn. You do. And we were.

We stopped in another rest stop and the guy invited me in for lunch. We had a half chicken, boiled potatoes and red cabbage washed down with a good beer. Damn. I hitch-hiked from St. Louis to California and back and ain't never had anything like this happen. The best I could make out from our conversation was that he was into heavy industry in the Ruhr Valley, which is why he's going to Essen.

When I get out of the car, I again thank him heartily and sincerely for the lunch and the ride. He just smiles, floors it and leaves me in a cloud of dust. I'm wondering if this is a fluke or could this happen again sometime. Before I can roll it around in my mind a couple of times, someone else stops. I didn't wait more than ten minutes between rides, all the way to Amsterdam. That's four hundred miles and changing three or four Autobahns. Many times did I make that trip and more than a few did I average sixty miles an hour. Incredible!!!

My last ride into Amsterdam that evening asked me where I wanted to get off. I said I didn't know because I'd never been here before. He looked me over and said he new just the place. In a few minutes I found myself standing on 'Dam Square,' looking up at a monument someone told me represented the victims that died in World War II. The Square itself was where the first inhabitants built a dam on the Amstel River. Hence the name Amsterdam and the center of the city.

Looked like something I'd never seen before. Full of people at ten o'clock in the evening, young people from all over the world. Some were dancing or playing music. Others sitting and watching or in animated conversations telling each other of their trips and experiences.

Joints were being passed around freely between different groups and all this in an atmosphere of freedom to express oneself as he wished. It was a menagerie of the mind that seemed surreal to me. I couldn't help thinking 'if this would happen in St Louis, the pigs would swoop down on everybody, beating the hell out of them and locking them up in jail---all the while saying "You can't do this kind of shit here, straighten up and get in line boy!!"

I looked around with some hesitation; this was too good to be true. And there they were, on a small side street just off the square, two policemen in a van watching everything that was going on. No binoculars, no cameras, just keeping an eye on things so they don't get out of hand. Two cops putting their time in with no threat to anyone. I like this place a lot already.

It was starting to get late and I was tired. I'd had an interesting day on the road, drinking in the scenery as it changed from rolling hills to the Dutch flat lands. Trying to see everything but going so fast it made you tired.

Black and white Holstein cows, lots of them, with endless green pastures to graze in. No fences to speak of, just small ditches with water in them to separate the fields which seemed to work well for the cows. I found out later those little ditches were two feet deep or more, so if a cow did step in them they'd be likely to break a leg. Cows knew it, so it worked. I couldn't help thinking of the old song "Don't fence me in."

The wide green landscape with no fences and a farm house here and there to mark civilization and a few puffy cumulous nimbus clouds on the horizon was the back drop of most all Dutch paintings, from the Great Masters until today. In that respect time had stood still.

The towns were easy to see in the distance. First was the church steeple on the highest spit of land at the center of town. That land had to have been built up because everything else around it was flat. Then the red-tiled roofed houses and businesses emanated out from the center of power and pivotal core, the church.

The roads approaching the old towns were like spokes on a wheel. No matter which way you entered, it was a straight line to the church. Just imagine coming to town with a horse and wagon and the main focal point for hours would be the church on the hill.

Today they come up fast and there's a definite line where the town ceases and the green pastures again take over the panorama. There is no urban sprawl. Even so, at eighty or ninety miles an hour and your eyes bouncing all over the horizon, it makes a guy tired. That's what I was, tired.

23. Cheap Sleeps

I started asking around for cheap places to stay. A few people told me about a couple of Dutch guys who had some old barges hooked together east of Central Station on the Prins Hendrikkade. They said the cost was two guilders per night, about sixty cents US, which was in my budget. Sounded cool and kind of romantic in a way, sleeping in a barge on the canals in Amsterdam. And I did a lot of that latter. But this time the reality was not like the dream-----it rarely is!

I walked there from the 'Dam' and went aboard the first barge. A guy was standing there pointing down an open hatch. I looked inside and saw a dim light and a ladder leading into oblivion. I flashed back to the ship from the Canaries with the Spanish paratroopers in the bilge. "Nah, this ain't happening again," I'm thinking.
I climb down the ladder and my eyes focus on row after row of triple layered steel bunks with about eighteen inches between them.

"Stacking them in pretty tight aren't ya." I said.

He replies "It's only two guilders a night; you want to go somewhere else?"
There's no second class to fight for and I'm beat. I look around to see a bunch of weary travelers, unkempt and carrying their dirty clothes around with them for weeks. The air is thick, stale and isn't moving, but at least there are no Spanish paratroopers.

"What's this?" The sweet smell of hashish and tobacco hits me. Joints are being passed around.

"What the hell," I said. "This will have to do." Handed him two guilders and grabbed a bunk close to the smoke. He just smiled.

I went to sleep with the sound of the bilge pumps kicking on every few minutes pumping the water out and keeping the old barge afloat. My last thought was "If there's a fire tonight, we're not all going to get out of here!" Pleasant dreams.

The next morning I gathered my stuff and my senses and got the hell off that barge. The first breath of fresh air had a taste of salt from the sea and a faint aroma of pickled herring. A lovely combination but a bit early in the morning for me. I passed the herring stand on my way to Central Station to get a sweet cake and a coffee. The sweet cakes throughout Europe were fantastic with each country having their own gourmet delights and the Dutch were not to be out done. The taste and variety were of the sort you'd never get tired of, with pastry shops no further apart than the time it took to eat one. So that many a time I'd be eating one sweet cake and looking through a window at the next.

I had my sweet cakes and coffee, grabbed my stuff and threw it into a locker, dropped a guilder in and turned the key. That was hard for me because for one guilder you could sit in a bar and have a draft beer like Heineken or Orangeboom. But sometimes it was worth it not to carry a bag.

Down the Damrak I go, it was the main street with back to back streetcars and busses going to and from Central Station. It was wall to wall people with lots of tourists in between because it was early summer now. Half way to the

'Dam' on the right was the American Express office. Most Americans traveling abroad used American Express traveler's checks. Their office also acted as a post office where travelers could pick up mail, meet other travelers and sell all sorts of things, such as cars, return airline tickets to the States or just about anything else you could imagine. The next couple of nights I spent in a place called the yellow door. The old barges were to the east of Central Station. The yellow door was to the west. On the same body of water which was the port. Amsterdam was built like a half moon or half circle with the Central Station at the northern end on the port and at the center. The Herren Gracht, Princen Gracht and the Keisers Gracht were the three main canals that followed the same semicircle route with all kinds of smaller feeder canals leading into the big three or the Amstel River.

Amsterdam was a city of the moment---yet timeless. The bridges, buildings and architecture seemed ancient to me. Still there were parts out of the 'Centrum' or center that were of a modern, avant-garde design. All the areas of which were lived in or worked in.

Warehouses converted to residential housing opening up right onto a canal where people came and went by small boat. The main 'signature' beam protruding out from the top of every building allowed the residents to move their furniture in and out by attaching a hook with ropes and pulleys. Reason being was the small winding stairwells going to the upper floors couldn't accommodate the furniture. Whether moving in or out, the movers would haul it up or down by swinging the goods through the large windows which always faced the street.

I saw a piano moved this way. It drew a small crowd of people. There seemed to be some doubt whether the beam would hold and the piano might drop down onto the cobblestones. The beam was well over two hundred years old. The piano as well, I believe. Everybody, including the movers were ready to run if the beam gave way. Half a dozen guys were reefing on the ropes to get it up there and when they swung the piano into the building there was shouting and a round of applause. Relief was written all over the faces of the movers.

I spent hour upon hour just walking and gaulking at the city.

~~~~

The yellow door was on the Haarlemmer Straat. Wasn't hard to find because,----yep, the big yellow door. You had to walk up a flight of steps to the second floor into a big room about the size of Volkers studio. Maybe sixty by thirty with mats like we had in gym class, all up and down each wall with a small isle to walk in the center.

For three guilders, or 90 cents US, you were allotted about three feet of space. That's it, no place to stash your stuff, everything out in plain view and the few couples with no sense of modesty who liked to share their passionate times together with everyone else were also amusing. You had to be really tired, to get a good nights sleep here. At least it had windows, air and that warm friendly glow of Amsterdam.

24. The Best of Cities

I loved to walk and gaulk at so many new sights and smells of the city. Something I never experienced before. A city so full of life and so many people, wall to wall people. Per square mile, Holland is the most populated country in the world. How they can all get along together is a triumph in toleration. The architecture made it seem like you were living in story book land. Mix in the glow from the hashish;--- and the bricks, cobblestones, bridges, boats, wooden shoes and copper towers made it all seem dreamlike.

Amsterdam was an eternal city, not like Rome, but for a Midwestern boy that had only seen a part of the States, it sure was. I was sleeping, eating and visiting in buildings older than the country I came from.

A city laid-out for the benefit of the people. Not for industry. You didn't need a car here. If the distance was too far to walk, bicycles were the norm. Everybody seemed to have one. They were everywhere. Hundreds in bike racks at the train stations or locked to posts or bridges. All single speed. I never saw a ten speed, not even a three speed. Course in flat lands you don't need them. Trouble was they were quiet. If you forgot to look before you stepped into the street and got nailed by someone on a bike in a hurry, you'd remember to look the next time! Guaranteed!

So much history, so much beauty, but what it really comes down to, no matter where you are, is the people.

The friendliest, most open and tolerant people I've ever met, and everybody ready to give a greeting or have a quick chat on the street.

For example: A friend and I go into a produce shop--- really stoned. The apples look fantastic. I pick one up and put it into my coat pocket. My friend rolls his eyes because he knows the shop keeper saw me. The shop keeper comes around behind me and takes the apple out of my pocket and puts it back on the stand. We walk out of the shop, I turn around and look at the shop keeper and slap the pocket where the apple was. We both point at each other and start laughing. He waves and off we go.

The next day I stop again at the shop and buy some fruit. We look at each other and smile knowingly. That's Holland. Now I'm no damn thief. I hate thieves. Hell, I don't know, I might have stolen that apple so I could tell this story.

~~~

Heading down the "Damrak" with a copy of the "Herald Tribune" under my arm, I stopped in front of the American express office. There was a crowd out front, mostly Americans. Some had signs trying to find rides somewhere, selling cars or waiting in line to check their mail.

I stopped for a minute to read the signs when someone grabbed me by the arm and swung me around. It was Frank. We greeted each other like long lost friends that hadn't seen each other in years. Of course it had only been a month or so, but both of us had experienced a lot. We sat and had a coffee and laughed about the times in Spain with

Rosita and the 'shit' in the toilet and the Nazi SS officer in Hamburg.

Frank told me he had a place in Paris, a fifth floor attic or atelier in the Latin Quarter where a lot of students hung out. His French was getting better and he was enjoying life. I told him what happened in Hamburg on the 'Reeperbahn' and how Volker and Kalley were doing.

We were all still alive and glad of it. Frank had to return to Paris that night so we said our goodbyes and hoped we'd see each other again. I did see him later----in the student riots in the summer of 1970 in Paris.

~~~~

The youth hostel in Amsterdam was like no other I'd ever stayed in. Certainly a far cry from the one in Tubingen where we were awakened with military marching music, where there was a place for everything and everything in its place. This was a rendezvous point for a lot of travelers---a place with a lot of drug dealers and a lot of 'big smoke' going on in the lobby. I stayed a couple of nights; it was clean and well run. And if you think those two sentences contradict each other, then,--- welcome to Holland.

Quint was selling hash in the lobby. He was a couple of years younger than me, with corduroy pants tucked into his tall black boots, long brown hair, brown eyes and a 'good face', always smiling. He'd tell me how good his shit was, roll up a nice joint and fire it up. We'd go back and forth bickering on the price like a couple of street vendors, smoking and laughing all the while. We hit it off well.

A few days later Quint introduced me to a friend of his named Eric. He was an art student, with long wavy hair that rested on his shoulders like a Ben Franklin wig. His nose was bigger than he liked and was accented by the large black framed glasses that sat on it. Said he had another room in his flat and I was welcome to stay for awhile. I thought that was a great idea.

    He lived on the Cornelius Van Troost Straat, about three blocks from the Heineken brewery. Every morning I'd walk down and catch the nine o'clock tour and when it was done, eat cheese and drink beer. That lasted until I corrected the tour guide. I new the tour as well as he did. Not smart, all that good Dutch cheese and Heineken beer and nobody counting how many you drank.

    Eric studied art at the University. The Dutch government would give art students with 'promise,' yearly grants. Each year they had to produce five or six painting the government would keep in a warehouse and should the artist make it big, those painting would be the property of the state, to sell and get their investment back. From what I saw, one day Eric would be renowned.

    He was a good friend who helped me when I needed it. His place was a refuge for those nights I made it back. I looked him up a year latter when I came back from the States and through him I met a girl that I'll never forget.

25. The "Big" Idea

Amsterdam is the hashish capitol of the world. Lots of young people passing through it on their way to or their way home from the East. The Eastern Mysticism magnet drew so many to Afghanistan, India and Nepal;--- all with fascinating, captivating stories. I longed to go there, but how to afford it? My money was getting low and I saw no way of replenishing it. Then I heard of an idea that sounded good.

Ya know when you travel alone you meet a lot of people. You have to if you don't want to be lonely all the time. Ya hear a lot of stories about where to go and where not to go, things and places to see and others to avoid. Ideas on how to make fast and easy money, those which succeeded and those which failed, but there was one idea that caught my attention.

It goes like this: Ya buy a car in Europe, take it to Turkey, sell it on the black market and make a thousand dollars clear. The thousand bucks put you back on easy street to continue your trip through Iran, Afghanistan, India and Nepal. Sound good? I thought so too.

Here's the catch. You enter Turkey from the West [Istanbul], sell the car and leave Turkey going East, into Iran. If you own the car when you enter and don't when you leave, the Turkish customs will charge you a thousand dollars because you obviously sold the car, which is the import tax on the vehicle. How do they know? When you entered Turkey, they wrote all this information in you passport and if they see it when you leave, without the car, you're busted.

If you were foolish enough to spend a lot of your 'new' money in Turkey and can't pay the duty if you get caught leaving, you'll sit in jail until they sort it all out.

The solution: Don't put the car in your name. The problem: You're driving all across Europe and into Turkey in a car you don't legally own. This seems workable. Especially after two months of continuous hashish and alcohol consumption to aid in my reasoning.

Hell, I did it from Kansas City to St. Louis without too much trouble. Besides, the Turks I met in Hamburg selling hash weren't all that smart. I can do this!

~~~~

That's when I met Ronnie and Olaf. They were at the bar in a night club called Paridiso, or Paradise. It was one of two famous clubs in Amsterdam. The other was the Melkweg, or Milky Way. Both were huge houses with multiple rooms and different scenes in each.

There was a room, like a typical Dutch bar, with that same type of patron; rooms with kaleidoscope light shows going on for the people tripping on acid. Smoking rooms full of people getting high on hashish and marihuana and a couple of rooms with a mélange of everything going on and all this with the express permission of the Dutch government.

Instead of a costly 'war on drugs,' the Dutch declared victory by quasi-legalizing soft drugs. They bust the big dealers but turned a blind eye on the small fish and everyday users. And lo and behold, their G.D.P hasn't diminished, their socio-economic system hasn't collapsed and forty years later there seems to be fewer drugs there now than when I lived there in the 70's.

Back to Ronnie and Olaf leaning against the bar having a beer. Ronnie was English from Birmingham and was short with brown hair and brown eyes that could have a penetrating stare when he wanted. He had a well made long leather coat with a wide belt and buckles, was about twenty-eight years old and on the mainland until things 'cooled-off' back home---a common denominator of those traveling for long periods of time. Look, anybody traveling longer than six weeks has a history, longer than that and they're wanted somewhere.

Olaf was a Hamburger. We hit it off right away because of my knowledge of the Repeerbahn and the seedier sides of Hamburg. Olaf was a couple of years older than me, a big guy, probably six foot six and about two hundred and eighty pounds. Real solid with light blonde hair, blue eyes and looked like he'd worked hard all his life and was tired of it.

We were all short of money. I told them about my idea and they were keen. Ronnie wanted to get further away from England and Olaf was more than willing to get lost in India for awhile.

We drank and smoked and tried to hash things out. No pun intended. Back and forth we went.

"How much money have you got?"

"How much do we need?"

"Where can we get a car?"

"In front of the American Express." I said. "We'll buy one from an American who's going home and get a good deal."

"What about the taxes?"

"Foreigners don't pay the tax unless they sell it to a local." I said. "I'm not putting the car in my name, how about you guys?
They just laughed.

"I know we have to get a green card for sure." I said. That's the insurance card, without that we're not crossing any borders!

I said "I'd get the info on the car tomorrow."

By the end of the night we had it figured out and it went like this: I'd buy the car. Ronnie had enough money to cover the food and Olaf would pay the gas. We were all pretty well screwed up so we decided to meet the next day and finalize everything.

I talked it over with a few friends to get their opinion and they said "You're crazy George, but it might work." I'd heard the first part before. It was the second part that I wanted to hear.

Did some research with a car rental agency and found out what they gave their clients to cross the border. I was told: the registration, which showed ownership and the green card, which was proof of insurance, has to be in the vehicle. They may or may not ask for the registration. But it's certain they'll ask for the green insurance card.

"Do you think they'll try to match up names on passports and car papers?" I asked.
The car rental agent just smiled and said "Good luck."

Met the boys the next day in Vondel Park as planned. Told them what I found out about the car and the borders and they were still keen. So I went car shopping out in front of the American Express. A girl with a sign advertising a 1962 VW bug for sale was in the crowd. She and her girlfriend had bought the car in Germany when they came over and had finished their trip and wanted to sell it before going home. I asked to see the papers. They looked to be in order. The registration was in her name along with the title and the green card had another two months left on it before it expired.

    The car was faded green with standard cloth seats. Everything worked on it and there were no big dings or scratches. To me, it was a winner.

    We went back and forth on the price. She wanted $350.00 but was in a weak position seeing how her flight was leaving in a couple of days. A 'bird in the hand' argument clinched the deal and we finally settled on $250.00 cash; which about cleaned me out. I had her sign over the title and registration to me. I might not appear to be the 'legal' owner of the car but I sure didn't want to be held as a car thief.

    My 'skin' was in the game and wanted to get going before the 'food' or 'gas' had too much time to think about it.

    I met Ronnie and Olaf later that afternoon and showed them the new acquisition. They weren't exactly thrilled, but what do you think you're going to get for $250.00. "This thing's going to make us a thousand dollars" I said. "Let's go!"

26. Heading Out

They went back to where they were staying, got their stuff and met me on the Leidseplein, near the Paradiso. Loading it up wasn't hard. We were traveling light. One bag each so we could grab it and run if necessary. I stopped for a few necessities; a case of beer and a nice piece of Red Lebanese hash. Around eight that evening we left Amsterdam---heading for Turkey.

Germany would be the first border we'd have to cross. Olaf was a bit nervous, something about the German Politzie instilling fear into the citizenry.

We drove South through Utrecht and Arnhem toward Emmerich where we'd cross the border. As we approached the booth I said "Okay, smiles everyone."

Damn, the Germans tried to match up the papers with the passports and when they didn't match, they refused us entry. Strike one.

"Well, we'll just have to try the next one." I said. "Maybe this guy was a little over zealous."

Tried the next crossing at Gennep, same story, the green card didn't have either of our names on it. Strike two.

Now Olaf and Ronnie start grumbling "Why did you buy a girl's car? Anybody in here look like a Jennifer, George?" says Olaf.

"Hey, piss-off Olaf, Ronnie doesn't, but you might pass for her. You want to drive?" I say.

"Maybe we're not going to get across." says Ronnie.

"Bullshit! "There's got to be some little farm road, cow path or some way we can cross over."

We drove down to the next check point at Venlo, which is a large crossing point. They checked our passports against the big book of registered criminals wanted by Interpol, looked at the green card and waved us through.

"Now we're talking," I said. But in the back of my mind I knew we still had to go along way. Austria was the next country we had to go through and they're no dummies either.

No time for sight seeing, we were on a mission. We drove pretty well straight across Germany stopping only for food and gas. Olaf and Ronnie were chipping in for food and gas, so they had a little 'skin' in the game now. The hash and beer were keeping spirits high since we got into Germany but Salzburg was just over the mountain where the next test would come. How would the Austrians greet us?

We pull up to the border and the guard takes our passports and hands them to his co-hart who checks them against the book. Then he sticks his head in to ask us where we're going and I see his nostrils flare. He might smell the hashish but I'm hoping the beer smell is over powering it. Hey, what the hell. We've just come out of Germany right?

They slug back more beer there, than anywhere in the world. So what's new? Let us in! I'm thinking. He gets our passports back from his mate and he asks to see the green card. Here we go! He gives us each a hard looking over, glances at the green card and waves us through. We're in on the first try. Things are looking up!

27. Tito's Yugoslavia

Again we drive straight through Austria on the Autobahn to the border with Yugoslavia. This is Tito's country. When the Germans were driven out at the end of the war, it was Tito who united these Balkan and Adriatic countries to repel the Russians and set up his own style of communism. He ruled with an 'iron fist' until he died.

There was no debate, no discussion, no where and at no time. Thousands would disappear. This was tyranny. You could read it on the faces of the people. I thought I sensed fear and apprehension in Franco's Spain, but this was deeper and more far-reaching.

We drove up to the check point where the steel gate was closed. We needed a visa to enter the country. The only kind you could get was a transit visa good for one week. The guard told us to park by the office and get out of the car, all of us. We had to fill out the forms in triplicate with no carbon paper. I wasn't real confident I could get them all identical. I doubted if they could read them anyway.

These guys had no air of professionalism like we'd experienced crossing the other borders. They were thugs. While we were inside filling out the forms, two other guys rifled through the car. I hoped they wouldn't find anything. They didn't. I caught them in the act when I came out and they didn't look very apologetic. I didn't push it. They were menacing. They wanted five bucks each for the visas. Since the food was costing less than the gas, Ronnie coughed up the money for the visas. As we were leaving I asked "Seven days, right?"

One guard just grunts.

"What if we break down and have to stay longer?" I ask The other guard comes over and gets in my face and says "Don't break down!" Intimidation was the rule of the day. We got in the car and drove away.

I was the only one with a driver's license. Ronnie had to leave his with the authorities in Birmingham. Olaf said something about not needing one because of good public transportation in Hamburg. I knew he was right. It was late now and I was beat. We'd come along way and there was a degree of mental stress crossing the borders. I pulled off onto a small road and then onto a dirt path leading into the woods.

We tried to sleep a few hours---the three of us in that little volks. Don't know which was worse, the crowding or the air. I thought the air in the barge in Amsterdam was bad, but this was a close second. And that's with the windows down. Well, one anyway. We were in a higher altitude and it was cold. Ronnie wouldn't open his even under protest from both of us.

~~~

I woke up to the sound of a horse snorting. Nahhh, I thought, but there it was again. I couldn't sleep any longer and got out quietly because the other guys were still snoozing. It was a crisp beautiful morning. The sun was creeping up over the hills on the horizon.

We had pulled in next to a field that was freshly plowed. A farmer was sitting on a harrow, pulled by a single huge work horse, breaking up the big clots and getting the field ready to plant. I'd seen this done in the States a few times with tractors, but never using horse power. As he came around again I waved and hoped he'd stop, but he just gave a slight nod of his head.

He stopped a little ways off and adjusted the harrow. He had an alpine style hat with no feather. When he took it off you could see it was well worn and held together by a few threads and revealed a white band across his forehead, the only part of his face protected from the sun. He wore a loose white peasant shirt; open at the neck and wool pants that were stuck into the tops of his black leather boots which looked like the kind the Russian soldiers wore in the war movies. I wanted to converse with the guy but he'd have no part of it. "Fear of the Tito Regime."

Now you might say I couldn't speak his language and you'd be right. But you can say a lot without speaking a word. I know, I'd been doing it for months now and getting along pretty well.

I was still all cramped up from sleeping in the car and decided to stretch my legs by taking a walk down the road. Came to a path going off into the woods and sat down on a large rock marking the intersection.

The beauty of the terrain, the fresh clean air and quiet solitude surrounding me was in stark contrast to the craziness of the last few days. I rolled a small joint of hash and tobacco, fired it up and took a moment of respite to reflect on what was, what is and what is to come.

I knew times like this would be a necessity for sanity in my life. I weighed the past. That was clear. The future was full of adventure and she was calling my name.

That's when I heard the whistle breaking the serenity of the moment. It was a bit shrill with a blast of turbulence pushing it from behind. There it was again, this time with a rolling thunder getting ever louder. Out of some deep recess of my mind came a faint familiarity of this sound but I couldn't put a finger on it. Then, from across the field and out of the forest, came an old locomotive pulling half a dozen freight cars.

I remember! "Petty Coat Junction," An out dated TV show that started with a locomotive rolling down the tracks, blowing its whistle with a couple of good looking girls on the engine. Damn.

No 'hotties' on this engine. She was black all over from the coal fired boiler and showed severe signs of abuse. The cow catcher in front was askew as if it had been used for that purpose more than once. The freight cars looked like the ones I'd seen in war movies getting blown up. Hell, if an airplane would have passed over I would have taken cover!

World War II ended twenty-five years ago and these guys were still using the same equipment. Gave me a pretty clear indication Communism wasn't keeping up. This didn't jive with the propaganda I heard form the commies at the University of Hamburg either.

The train woke Ronnie and Olaf up. They were looking for me and I met them about half way to the car. Neither of them had noticed the farmer and shrugged off the steam locomotive as if it was no big deal. I was impressed, a step back in time. I saw this stuff in museums!

Years later I was at a county fair which was having a demolition derby with farm combines. My cousin Terry almost won. While she was smashing and crashing I thought "We could sell everyone of these in Yugoslavia."

We were laughing and clapping at their destruction. Only in America!

~~~

We loaded back into the car and headed off down the Autobahn which ran though the central corridor of the country; the straightest route to Greece. Passing first through Zagreb, Belgrade and finally Skopje with Greece, the cradle of civilization for the western world, dead ahead.

We'd been cramped up and sleep deprived in this little volks long enough to put everybody's nerves on edge. Ronnie flipped when I asked him "What?" for the tenth time in the last two minutes.

"Can't you speak fucking English?" He asks

"Hell yes. Is that what you're speaking? I hear the words but they don't make sense. Are you stupid or what?" He had a thick Birmingham accent with a lot of local idioms that just didn't translate into 'Midwest American.' I found out later, nobody else in England could understand that accent either.

Olaf was dead quiet, starring forward and showing no emotion like a ticking time bomb with a short fuse. I didn't even see him blink. Might as well have had a sign around his neck saying 'don't mess with me!'---and I didn't. The vibes were heavy, nearing explosive. If we all started swinging in the car no telling how it would turn out.

28. Toes

Zagreb wasn't far; when we got there we parked the car and split up for a few hours. I bought a bottle of wine and a small sausage and sat on the edge of a fountain in the main square. Took off my boots, stuck my feet in the water, took a swig of wine and cut off a piece of sausage. Things were looking up.

Bozo, pronounced Bow Show, walks up and stands near the bottle of wine. He's about six feet six with a two inch scar on his left cheek. Brown eyes, brown hair and a strong build; he's wearing worn army fatigues with the standard issue black leather boots. Looking pretty hard at my wine so I offer him the bottle and he takes a big swig. Hands it back, takes his boots off and sticks his feet in the water to cool off as well.

We pass the bottle back and forth washing the sausage down until they're both done. He sees my knife and makes a gesture for it. I give it to him and he checks the edge for sharpness. Pulls one foot out of the water and puts it on the edge of the fountain and sets about trimming his toe nails.

Now the weak and meek might say "Oh gross" but hell, I'm fascinated. I never used anything else but a toe nail clipper, you know the right tool for the right job.

I start laughing and he looks at me funny but there's no way to explain. When he's done with his other foot I notice mine could use a little work too. If he could do it, I guess I could too and gave it a try. It worked, wasn't any pedicure by any stretch, but I knew from this day on if I had to, I could cut my toe nails with a knife. I doubt if I'll learn anything like this at school next semester.

Two policemen were watching us from across the square. I discretely point them out to Bozo. He nods and says the only two English words I'll hear him say "Fuck them!" I return a wry smile and a nod in agreement.

We communicate as best we can. I understand him to say he's just finished two years of mandatory military service in Tito's army. I tell him I'm going to have to do the same thing in the States. He shakes his head and slaps me on the shoulder and says "Vietnam." I raise both arms and hands with palms up as to say "What choice is there?" I didn't get a clear meaning from the shaking of his head when he said Vietnam, but probably all the possibilities will work. I think he has empathy for me.

We put our boots back on and he shows me a good cheap restaurant a couple of blocks away. We split up then. I wish him well and mean it not knowing the hell Bozo will probably go through during the split up of Yugoslavia. And to think he shows concern about me and Vietnam. What a world!

I met up with Ronnie and Olaf soon after splitting off from Bozo. We went to the restaurant he showed me and had a great, cheap meal. Loaded back into the little volks and headed South toward Belgrade. Drove right through the capitol and still couldn't miss some of the stunning architecture prevalent in the city. Time was of the essence.

The words of the border guard 'thug' were ringing in my ears "Don't break down." We drove for hours until the wine and hash won the battle for sleep. I pulled down a side road for awhile and into an open field of winter wheat.

It was late, pitch black and not a single light on the horizon. "Nobody will bother us here" I said and fell asleep.

29. May Day

We slept for what seemed like ten minutes, but really was four hours. I'm dead to the world and it's dead quiet when somebody starts banging on the car and yelling. Somebody is walking around the car and banging on the sides and the top yelling something---who knows what? Shit, what a way to wake up! If they could make an alarm clock like that, nobody could sleep in.

We get out of the car. It's still dark, on the horizon is a faint glow, dawn can't be far off. With all the commotion and banging on the car I'm thinking there's a half a dozen guys out here and I'm about to get my ass kicked.

It's one guy, a farmer; short with shabby loose fitting clothes, a big black mustache and he's pissed-off royally. He's pointing at the ground, waving his arms and carrying on like a mad man. I can see I rolled over some of the wheat but couldn't help but think, damn, they'll probably stand up when we pull away. What's the big deal?

I shouldn't joke; it is a big deal to him. The 'commies' have never been able to feed themselves and now I just killed a few stalks of wheat.

We start talking to him and he realizes we're all foreigners. He can't make out a word of what Ronnie and I are saying, but he's smiling. We're making progress here until Olaf says something to him in German. The farmers' countenance changes. He says something to Olaf, still no smile. I look at Olaf and ask "What the hell did you say?" Olaf looks at me and says "Nothing, I think it's about the war."

Seems the old boy doesn't have very good memories about the German occupation and still holds hatred for the Germans. I understand, I've been treated rudely a few times because of my country's role in Vietnam.

Time to get the farmer's mind onto something else; Ronnie and I both start talking, waving our arms and take a step closer to him leaving Olaf in the back ground. He's smiling again and makes a gesture to wait---wait right here. Walks about fifty feet away and picks up two big bundles of something. Comes back over and in the early morning light, I can make out two wicker covered glass jugs.

He sits one down and throws the other up onto his shoulder and takes a big swig. You can hear the bubbles going back up into the jug, swings it off his shoulder and hands it to Ronnie.

Homemade wine, ten or twelve gallons at least, Ronnie passes it to me. It's good! We pass it between the three of us a couple of times leaving Olaf out. I'm starting to get a glow and when the old boy has the bottle up I look at Olaf and wag my finger at him saying

"The sins of the fathers pass on to the next generation." Of course, I get the 'screw you' look from Olaf.

I get the picture! Took long enough, but hey, it's five in the morning and I've already got a glow on. The farmer's on his way to the big Mayday Festival. It's May 1st. It's the day of celebration for the proletariat.

"Workers of the world unite. We have nothing but our chains to loose. Let the ruling classes tremble at a Communist Revolution!" We drink a few more rounds to the revolution and he invites us to go to the festival. I don't think the invite includes Olaf, either way we decline graciously, time and again.

We say our goodbyes and he heads off toward town. I look back from where he came and could just make out a small light from a hut at the edge of the woods. Probably kerosene by the amount of light it gave off.

Nice of him to invite us to the party, I hope he has a great time. Just can't help thinking to myself "I'm a capitalist; I bought this car with capital and plan to make a tremendous profit on it I hope. I probably wouldn't be welcome at the party.

We loaded back into the car and headed off to find something to eat. Felt a pang of guilt as I ran over a few more stalks of wheat in the farmer's field, but we had to get out of there somehow.

30. The Cradle of Western Civilization

The early start was a boost for us because we arrived at the border with Greece at a normal hour instead of the middle of the night. They checked our passports and the green card but didn't bother to match up the names. We made it in slick and easy, only the Turkish border remained and we were all confident.

We rolled into Thessaloniki in the early evening. Saloniki, as the Greeks call it, was built on a hillside sloping toward a big bay on the Aegean coast where the white stucco homes and businesses accented the deep blue water of the Aegean Sea.

The second largest city in Greece and at one time, second only to Constantinople way back in the day, looked now like another one of the laid back Greek towns we'd been driving through all day, only bigger. This was the land of baklava, gyros, souvalaki and a history that goes back to day one.

Alexander the Great was born about twenty miles northwest of here. We'll be driving by his place tomorrow when we head toward Turkey.

The dry, rough and dusty roads we'd been traveling on gave me a powerful thirst. One I wasn't sure I could quench, but more than willing to try. Besides, this was a time for celebration. We just drove a car all the way from Amsterdam that we didn't legally own, no mean feat I'd say.

Pulled into the first café we came to. This was my first introduction to Ouzo. A strong liquor flavored with anise, when mixed with water, would turn cloudy like Pernod.

It's got about forty percent alcohol and should come with a warning label. Retsina is the local wine, red and white. Both have a strong taste of pine resin and with the first swig are hard to get over the palate. But when accompanied with a shot of Ouzo, with or without water, seems to cut the pine resin like a blow torch on pine sap and allows it to flow freely down the gullet. Once the process is started, only wisdom and common sense can stop it. And they lose influence with each shot.

The locals suggested the brand of Ouzo and white Retsina. Guaranteed to loosen up our tired aching muscles and joints, tongues, bowels or whatever other affliction we might have. 'Medicine of the Gods' they said. I still had a piece of hash so things couldn't have been better. We started self-medicating!!!

The people were warm and friendly. The more we drank, the better it got. We ate good food that I'd never had before and danced in circles until the place closed; then slept in the car again because none of us thought to get a hotel. Kind of like a dog that's comfortable sleeping in it's own crate!

Sleep came easy with a sweet spirit of knowing the conquest of our mission was at hand. We'll be in Istanbul tomorrow where all things will be beautiful and fall into place to continue our trip east.

The next morning when I woke up------I was hurt! Those aching muscles and dust covered tongue from the rough roads the day before were nothing compared to what was going on inside my head this morning. I didn't know where I was or what I did last night. If death was close I would have beckoned him on.

That faded vision of conquest I had last night was now eclipsing into a deep hole of defeat. And who the hell is playing the big bass drum in my head?!!!

The memories of the night before started easing in after a couple of cups of ill appreciated, but excellent coffee. We gathered up the pieces, had a shot of the 'hair of the dog' to keep the car between the ditches and headed off to Turkey where dreams of money and adventure were waiting.

31. No Man's Land

It was about two hundred miles to the border and by the condition of the roads we were on; it was going to be awhile. That's fine, because if I look the way I feel right now we might have a problem getting in. It's been a hard few days, but in four or five hours I'll be ready to start again.

Which brings to mind; I can't remember the last time I saw myself in a mirror. I looked my compatriots over and hoped I didn't look as bad as them. They looked like they were pissed at and missed and shit at and hit; smelled that way a bit too. By the time we got to Alexandropoulos our spirits were raising with anticipation as we drew near the Turkish border.

We drove up to the Greek border and the guards were friendly enough. Most countries don't care what you take out; it's what you bring in! As we were waved through I asked "Where's the Turkish Border?" The guard just pointed down the road. I couldn't see anything but desert and scrub brush. All the borders I'd ever crossed before were lines with each country's guard houses right next to each other. We were now in "No man's land." A new experience for me; I'd heard the term before but now it was taking on a whole new meaning.

Seems the Greeks and Turks don't get along very well. Never have. Fifty years earlier Solaniki was Turkish. They've been fighting for centuries, actually more like millenniums and no end in sight. They just call a halt to it for awhile until one side gets a little stronger than the other and then start again, like the Island of Cypress; half Greek and half Turkish. There was a lull now and we were hoping to take advantage of it.

I could see the guard house coming into view. All around was wide open space with excellent visibility. I recall someone saying last night that it would be impossible to drive around the guard house because of the mine fields. I don't remember studying this in school; should have paid better attention I guess.

We pulled up to the Guard house. There were four of them and they all got up to greet us. 'How nice.' Three of them had a similar look. Tall thin and with big black mustaches; uniforms which were obviously not their prime concern. These guys were just putting in their time.

The guy doing the talking was different. He was short with squared back shoulders, impeccable uniform and of course a big black mustache that was well trimmed. He spoke English very well with an Oxford accent which seemed comical at the moment but one snicker or laugh I 'm afraid would have put us in jeopardy. This guy was all business.

"Everybody out" he says.
Since I was driving, he pulled me aside and asks "Is this your car?"

"Yes sir."

"Papers"

I give him my passport, green card and registration jumbled up together, hoping he'd look at the mess and let us go; but not this guy. He collects Ronnie and Olaf's passports, glances at his cohorts with a 'this is how it's done' look and sets about checking our papers. Takes each passport, stares at the picture and looks at the owner. Then turns each page slowly looking for some hidden wrong he might reveal.

My hopes were starting to fade, but you can't let him see or sense it. Lot's of eye contact going on and I wasn't going to be the first to blink. Ronnie and Olaf were holding their own as well. I mean this is it! We've got solid resolve here. We've come along way for just this moment. I don't know if my buddies have given it any thought as to what we'd do if we can't get in. I know I didn't, but the possibility was looming.

I'm looking at this guy and thinking 'how out of place he is here' especially compared to the other guards. This guy is Mr. Officious, probably out from the head office today to check on the forlorn outposts of the empire. Maybe shake-up and instill some fear into his subordinates. Why did we have to drive up at this moment?

He's checking all the papers methodically. Of course the names on the insurance card and registration are not matching up with any of our passports. The questions are getting louder and more intense. He says "You told me this car is yours. Why is it not in your name?"

I start giving him the lame story about buying the car in Amsterdam from an American girl and since she had to leave on a plane right away we didn't have time to validate the papers.

Times like this you speak in circles and try to get the guy confused and frustrated because it's his second language and just maybe he'll say 'the hell with it' and let you go. But not this guy, his English is better than mine and he's not buying my story. This is not good.

"You are lying!"

"You want to sell this car here in Turkey!" He says.

"No no no" I say with my arms out from my sides, palms up and the 'dumb American' look on my face.

"You think we're stupid! You're not the first do this, others have tried and they are in jail!"

He opens each of our passports and puts the stamp of the country in them and a big X over it. We've just been deported or refused entry into Turkey. Either way we're screwed! He hands back our passports and says "You have been refused entry into Turkey. If you try to enter again, anywhere, you will be caught and held for questioning."

Damn!##@#%#!#$%##!!!$%&%#

We got back in the car, turned around and headed back to Greece. It was a relief to be in the car and driving away from what seemed like a near miss at doing some jail time. Emotions are running high. Our vision of money and good times has just collapsed. Now, another slap in the face comes when I think 'my God, will the Greeks let us back in?' They have to know something is wrong. What if they check the car papers? I don't say anything about it, but the silence in the car is deafening. We must all be wondering if we're going to be stuck in 'no man's land'.

It's looking a whole lot drier, more desolate and uninviting than when we came through the first time. The quip about the minefields last night flashes through my mind again. 'Lord have mercy.'

The Greek guard house appears and I'm sure we're all silently praying. I know I am. He's looking at us as I hand him our passports through the window. Checks the pictures against the faces and waves us on, didn't even ask for the green card. "What's up with that?" I'm thinking. The guard has to remember us; we were just here an hour ago, unless they had a change of shift or something.

Maybe the prayer worked. I know I'm thankful to be back in Greece.

32. Back in the West

Back in Solaniki we had been sleeping in an olive grove on the edge of town. A café was near and the youth hostel was in easy walking distance. Down but not out; we sat and brain-stormed off and on for a couple of days, not really coming up with any good ideas.

The money problem was rearing its ugly head again. Ronnie and Olaf were doing better that I because the cost of the car about wiped me out, but they knew they couldn't hang on here for long.

Ronnie showed up with a newspaper add seeking mercenaries for Israel. We hashed it over for awhile. Said they're paying five hundred pounds per month for foreign soldiers. I said "Hell, that's a thousand dollars a month, maybe we could tough it out for a month?" They're not at war right now, if we keep our heads down and duck out of as much work as possible, it might be done. We went back and forth. One month, just one month.

You know they're going to have us do the worst and most dangerous crap because we're mercenaries. Then I looked at Olaf and said "Hey man, being German they might give you some real easy stuff to do." Ronnie and I started laughing. Olaf gave me the finger. He's learned that on this trip and uses it effectively.

I took a closer look at the add. The five hundred pounds weren't sterling, or English, they were Israeli pounds, about sixty bucks. "No thanks."

The 'gig' was up. Olaf was the first to leave. He was almost broke. It was up to him to pay the gas and since we weren't going anywhere he thought his best chance was to head out while he still had something. I couldn't blame him. Ronnie was next. Same story, but he was buying the food and what little he had left would go a lot further spending it on him than sharing it with me; again no hard feelings.

So there I was. Stuck in Thessalonica with no money and a car I didn't legally own. The hash was gone too. "What the hell happened?"

Pissing and moaning wasn't going to help. I was getting hungry, so I got busy. First I tried the youth hostel, talking to everybody passing through and trying to get them to buy the car. Had a few nibbles but as soon as they found out the papers weren't in my name they shied away.

I slept on the floor of the youth hostel underneath a bed on a lower bunk for a few nights until the management caught on.

The evenings turned out to be a plus. The Greeks have a 'happy hour' as well. They gather at the cafes and restaurants around five and drink ouzo and retzina. While they drink they always have something to eat; little snacks such as garbanzo beans, bread, olive oil, tomatoes and onions, deep fried calamari or feta cheese or any number of things.

I'd walk into these places alone. When you're alone it's always easier to meet people. There'd be a couple of guys at a table relaxing and having a drink, thankful their work day was done. They'd see me, nudge each other, call me over, push out a chair and buy me a drink. Communication was tough. Most couldn't speak but a few words of

English and I could only say 'please and thank you' but that didn't stop us from trying.

A lot of times I knew they were making fun of me which didn't bother me because I was eating all their snacks. When the snacks were all gone, I'd get up, shake their hands, slap them on the back and go to the next café and do it all over again, until 'happy hour' was over.

I lived like that for days. Sleeping in the olive grove at night and trying to sell the car in the day. Since the car wasn't registered in Greece I couldn't sell it to a Greek. The import tax killed the deal. It had to be a foreigner. I went to the US consulate. Should be some foreigners there, right? Tried talking to a few people but no one was interested. They were all living to well to buy an old car.

The consulate heard I was trying to sell a car without a title and came up to me and said "You can't sell that car here and if we hear that you have, we'll notify the Greek authorities and have you prosecuted."

Prosecuted, He said. Prosecuted! I've been prosecuted for drinking a beer with my friends; prosecuted for having empty beer cans in my car; prosecuted for rolling a stop sign. No wonder our jails are full. And now they still want to prosecute me here in somebody else's country at one of the lowest points in my life. "Oh say can you see, by the dawns early light," how helpful our diplomatic corps is to its' citizens!!

33. *Blood Money*

I heard the hospital and the Red Cross were buying blood. The hospital was paying sixteen dollars; the Red Cross eight. I went to the hospital first. In the waiting room were about twenty five people already signed up and waiting to sell. Trouble was you had to wait until someone needed your blood before they would buy it. Since I had a 'Plane Jane' blood type of A+, which was as common as fleas on a dog, my chance of being called was slim to none. The way I was feeling, if I waited a few more days, even the Red Cross might not buy it.

That was my next stop, the Red Cross. It was a small building right on the waterfront next to the port and across the street from a café. I walked in; they looked me up and down and knew what I was there for. I filled out the forms, they walked me over and laid me down on a gurney and started the I.V. They'd come by and check the flow every once and awhile.

The gurney was pretty comfortable and I nodded-out thinking of how I was going to spend my eight dollars. I woke up to a little excitement around my bed. Seems they took more blood than intended. I asked if I could be paid more money for the extra blood, but nobody laughed. They gave me some orange juice and told me to lay down for awhile. I did, but neither rest nor sleep would come.

I was paranoid they might not pay, but they did; eight dollars worth of Greek drachmas. Now, with a little 'coin of the realm' in my pocket, things were looking up. I walked across the street to the café, had two shots of Ouzo, walked across to the docks, sat down and passed out.

~~~~

It was getting dark when I woke up with an awful acid burn in my stomach. Thought I was dreaming about selling my blood until I reached into my pocket and felt the money. It was true!

There was a little restaurant up the street. The menu might as well have been Greek, Oh yeah, it was! You couldn't make out anything; from street signs, local maps or menus.

The owner's wife came over to take my order. I looked at the menu, raised my hands in a "What's this gesture?" and she waved me back into the kitchen where her husband, in a white apron, starts raising the lids on the pots sitting on the stove. I pointed at this, this, and this. He explained what each was, but I couldn't understand a word. Yet it was the best meal I had in weeks. Fantastic!

The car still had a little gas, but I didn't want to drive it because I had a feeling like something might break and then it would be worth nothing.

34. Voices from on High

The elation from the meal was fading as fast as my money. The next day I found myself in a deep funk, sitting by the car, looking out to sea. The sun was sinking down below the horizon; a good depiction of how my life was sinking down as well. I had my head in my hands and said to no one in particular "Oh God, what am I going to do now?"

With that, I hear a "Hey man," from behind me. It's the kings English. I looked up to see two guys walking toward me. Both had white button down shirts with collars and carrying sport coats. One had kaki shorts and the other long pants. The one in pants was tall with curly black hair he parted on one side and tried to comb to the other, without much success. The other was a head shorter with brown hair and brown eyes. Both looked like they just stepped off the bus from some English prep school. I was a little apprehensive.

The next thing I hear is "Hey man, do you know where we can buy a used car?"

I immediately jump up and start doing a jig around my car and finish with a Fred Astair stomp and a 'feature presentation' wave at the car, "Right here my friends!" They looked at me like I might be a bit crazy and at the time they might not have been that far off.

I said "Really man, the volks is for sale."
They asked how much? I said $300 US. We went back and forth on the price and I realized these guys were serious buyers. We settled on $250. I was elated, but

hadn't dropped the bomb yet. They said "There's one Problem."

"What's that," I said as the sun starts going behind the clouds.

"Our car broke down in Yugoslavia; we scrapped it there and can only pay you in Yugoslavian 'dinars'." I knew the dinars were no good in Greece or anywhere else for that matter. I thought "What the hell, at least I'd have a great time in Yugoslavia." Since they had their own little bombshell I dropped mine next. "I've got a problem too." The tall one raised an eyebrow. "I don't have a proper title for the car."

They look at each other. My hope starts to wane. The tall one said "No problem man, we have one from the car we scrapped in Yugoslavia." I can't believe this. We walked down the street until we find a shop with a typewriter. Using hand signals I ask if we can use it?

Graham is the tall one; we've made the normal introductions by now and Steve is the short one. Graham sits down in front of the typewriter and rolled in their old title, comes to the space where the type of car is indicated and X's out Citroen and types in Volkswagen,---just like that. I cracked up. I like these guys a lot already!! It was a combination of surreal exuberance and knowing the tide had turned, my ship was here.

I had a wad of Yugoslav dinars the size of which would choke a horse and a bright future ahead. I knew I'd change those dinars some way.

We parted company. They headed off in their 'new' car toward Athens where we hoped to meet again. I was going to hitch-hike there via Delphi as soon as I could change the money. The best place to start was the youth hostel; trading dinars for Greek drachmas to young people leaving Greece for Yugoslavia. Of course you had to give the Americans a good deal because of their inbred paranoia that somebody was always out to cheat them.

It took a couple of days, but I finally got it done. I had $220 US in Greek drachmas which I took to a bank and got another shock. The banks wouldn't change their own money into US, pounds, deutschmarks or whatever unless you could prove where you got the money. That was out. Again it looked like I'd at least have a good time in Greece.

I was celebrating my good fortune in a seedier part of town near the port when two guys came stumbling out of a bar right in front of me. One says to the other in slurred American English "We've got to get some more 'drachs'." I said "Hey you guys, maybe I can help you. The banks are closed but I've got some extra 'drachs'. We went back into the bar they just came out of where I met a lot more American sailors on liberty from their ship in the harbor. The bar keep was charging them a hefty rate of exchange for their dollars. I charged them a little less. We drank beer, swapped stories and money and I walked out of there with $250 US. Back on top!

The next day was slow hitch-hiking. The hot and dusty dirt roads made it worse. Cars passed by pretty seldom with just enough time between them to build up some enthusiasm and hope; only to be dashed in a cloud of dust. Any time now I knew my big ride would come but it didn't happen. Only small rides for a few kilometers, even a tractor and wagon.

Before leaving Solaniki I met two Americans returning from Nepal. They had some fantastic hash which they planned to sell in Amsterdam to help pay their trip. Another good idea! I bought ten dollars worth; about thirty grams. After telling me a number of stories about their trip I was sorry the Turks were so thorough in checking our papers. Hell, I would have probably been there by now.

35. Delphi

On the long dusty road to Athens, I met a guy named Pieben from the town of Aalborg in the Jutland which is the main stretch of land north of Germany sticking into the North Sea.

Once he said Aalborg, I felt we had something in common. The famous Danish snaps are made there of which I'd already had a few notable episodes, if you recall, and would one day lead me deep into a Spanish dungeon--- but that's latter. Pieben had blonde hair past his ears, with blue eyes and a strong build. I listened intently to his stories of Denmark and the beautiful girls, knowing one day I would be there.

We were waiting in the shade for a ride, with lots of time and nothing to eat or drink. I rolled a nice joint and we got a good buzz on. A farmer, on a tractor pulling a wagon, waved to us to jump on as he passed by. He slowed down just enough for us to be able to make the leap on board with our gear. For the next half hour we watched the orange and lemon groves pass slowly by. As he made his turn into a lemon grove, Pieben and I jumped off the wagon, waved a big thank you and started walking down the road.

It was time to re-ignite the buzz, but I couldn't find the hash. I realized I left it back where we jumped on the farmer's wagon. During that long dusty walk back I made a vow that would never happen again.

We stopped by Delphi for a day and checked out the ruins; truly the most impressive and beautiful in all Greece.

Ancient, incredible history at your finger tips. If only one had a time machine to turn back, and see the "the great, the noble" coming form around the known world to seek wisdom from the Oracle. Maybe if I had some LSD left from the pop-festival in Hamburg I could have witnessed something like that, but who knows how accurate that would be! We looked, but couldn't find the Oracle, so we headed for the café.

There was a construction crew working on a road with a beautiful view of the valley. A big strong guy was using a jack hammer on a stubborn out-cropping of rock. The dust and rock chips hung heavy on his sweat soaked clothes. He stopped the hammer and looked up as I touched his shoulder. Pointing at my eyes, then across the vast panorama of the incredible valley I made the gesture for "magnificent." He in turn waved his arm over the view, pointed to his eyes, shook his head and pointed down at the jack hammer and started back to work.

I saw him later in the café and we had a drink together. Conversing as best we could, I went away with the impression that Pappadopolous, the American supported dictator, was not very popular with the workers. It was sad to think, with so much beauty around, that for some, there was no time to appreciate it. Another example of "keeping your nose to the grinding stone."

Pieben and I slept in the ruins at Delphi and headed toward Athens in the morning. It was only a trip of about a hundred miles, but it took all day. We arrived at dinner time. Hitch-hiking in Greece was not like hitch-hiking in Germany, by any stretch.

Pieben wanted to go to the Youth Hostel to make sure he had a place to sleep. We'd heard they filled up fast. I wasn't so sure. Youth Hostels can be pretty restrictive, but I said I'd take a look.

We arrived just as dinner was being served. Spaghetti with meat sauce, but if there was any meat in the sauce, I couldn't see it and it was cold to boot! The only good thing was, it was cheap. We were hungry and tired, so we dug in.

Sitting across from me was a dirty, greasy, skinny guy with black teeth and a bad smell. The plate in front of him was as empty as the look in his eyes. Something caught my attention across the room and when I turned to look, 'black teeth' reached for my bread.

I caught his movement out of the corner of my eye and stabbed down hard with my fork into his hand. It felt like it sank in deep and by the way he cried out in pain, it must have. He grabbed his hand and ran out, leaving his empty plate. I hadn't had anything to eat since early in the morning and wasn't going to let that slime ball steal my dinner.

36. Athens

I figured it best not to hang around the Youth Hostel after that incident. We said our goodbyes and I grabbed my bag and headed out to see Athens. More culture shock. I love it.

The change was dramatic, from the laid-back and relaxed rural Greece, where the mandatory evening 'promenade' after dinner showed off the pretty, prettier and prettiest girls in town. Walking right behind them would be their parents and grand parents, keeping an ever vigilant eye on them and their young suitors trying to make their moves. It was pure and unadulterated street theater. Life in the sticks!

From there, I was in downtown Athens; a city with too many people in too big a hurry and too busy to look up at the hills around them which are capped with ancient relics and ruins dating back to antiquity. If you stopped, you'd better be in a doorway, or expect to be bumped and jostled.

I was caught-up in thinking about the wonders of the ancient world, when a modern one almost ran me down. A city bus; a wonder in itself, to see how many people could fit in and on one. The doors were open front and back, people hanging on everywhere, heads and shoulders out the windows calling to friends or acquaintances as they passed. One bus after another, every few minutes, running in all directions.

I had a few drinks in different cafés trying to find out where the young people hung out. Monastraki square was the place. There had been an ancient monastery here, but now the square was full of cafés and shops. I met some interesting people as always. Mostly young travelers like myself having come from or going to the Greek Isles; usually Mykinos, Crete, Corfu or Rhodes. As I heard the stories about these places, a strong desire to visit them loomed over me.

The Retsina and Ouzo were beginning to take a toll. It was getting late and I needed a place to crash. A guy named Jost from Holland was in a group of people I'd been talking with and he said he was going up to the Acropolis to sleep in the ruins. It sounded good to me, so I tagged along.

The Acropolis is a limestone hill with very little dirt. We climbed almost to the top, looking for a flat place; not easy to find. When we did, there were rocks everywhere. No matter which way you rolled there was a rock in your back. I don't know of anybody that spent more than a few nights up there. Waking up to the view of Athens below made it almost tolerable.

At night, they closed the tourist route up the Acropolis to the Parthenon and Erechtheion leaving the whole place to a few of us travelers who would drink wine, catch a buzz and discuss the wonders of the ancient world right below our feet.

The guards in 1970 were non existent or couldn't care less and besides, what were we going to do that hadn't been done here for over a thousand years anyway. Even today, when I hear people speak of the Parthenon I can't help but think "Hell, I used to sleep up there."

Beautiful as it was in the morning, there was a long walk to get a much needed coffee. The fastest route was straight down and after all the wine and smoke from the night before, it's a wonder we didn't take a bad fall.

Jost went on his way and I went into a café right across the street from an ancient church. While having that much needed coffee and eating a yogurt with honey, I studied the old church. When I walked onto the street, the church drew my attention. As I looked at it, all things around me seemed to fade out, even the sounds of the city dissipated. The thought came to me that the apostle Paul preached here at some point.

I remember a Bible story about two guys casting out demons from possessed people. The demon asked them who they were. When they answered, the demon said he knew Peter and Paul but not them and set about beating the crap out of those two guys. Anyway, I was having some kind of spiritual experience. Maybe some overlapping of time or what, but to me it was intended to be significant. How exactly, I don't know. It's as vivid today as it was then. And no, no, it wasn't the hash. I knew that buzz ever so well. This was a much higher phenomenon. Wait, that was in Ephesus, hmmmm, ---hash?

37. A Way Back North

I went by the Youth Hostel to see if Pieben was there. He was gone but Graham and Steve just got in from Thessalonica. The first recognition between us was joy, the second---they were pissed off. Seems they got about twenty miles outside of Thessalonica when a valve went through a piston. They had to wait ten days for the parts. I pleaded 'not guilty' due to ignorance of mechanics. It ran fine when we cranked it up during the test drive and sale.

I must have been convincing enough, because we left the Youth Hostel for a café and had a couple of beers while we swapped stories of what had happened to each other in the last couple of weeks. They were heading back to England in a day or two. The repair bill must have put a dent in their traveling budget. I was pondering going to the Isles but with a ride back north staring me in the face, who could resist? My offer to kick in for gas, at least up to Paris, cinched the deal.

Two days later I was riding high in the backseat of the old volks, with a case of beer and the hash from Nepal.

Steve and Graham were in a hurry to get home. We drove pretty well straight through to the border with Yugoslavia. Bought our transit visas and the border guards didn't seem to have a problem with the x'ed out car names on the title.

In Macedonia near Skopje, up in the higher elevation, the car broke down. There was a thick fog with zero visibility. Somebody passed us by driving a horse cart with rubber car tires. I could here a village up the hill a little further.

Graham started jacking up the car, Steve pulled out a red tool box that opened on the top and had four slid out drawers full of tools. It looked like a professional tool box you'd see in a garage. Where did this come from? I thought. Those guys rolled up their sleeves and started to work. They popped off the valve cover on one side and started adjusting something. I said "there's no use me hanging around here, I'll be up at the town."

Picture this. I walk up the hill to find a village consisting of two stores and a bar set in a deep fog. I could hardly see fifty feet. The horse cart that passed us on the road is tied up to a store-front and the farmer is loading large sacks of grain. The fog and cold dampness in the air seems to go right to my bones. Maybe a shot of Slivovitz [plum brandy] might help, I thought; couldn't hurt, so into the bar I go.

The bar is about eighteen feet long. One guy is leaning on the far end and a couple of locals are at a table. Everybody is staring at me, no sweat, I'm used to it. I order a Slivovitz and throw it back, the heat starts taking over from the cold so I order another.

The door opens and in through the fog walks a big guy with a gun slung over his shoulder. He's wearing a wool cap with a short bill and a red star in the center. His broad face, bushy eyebrows, mustache and deep set eyes give him a Josef Stalin look. The mud all over his black military boots tells me he's got no ride and must be walking. He's walking alright, he's doing the rounds, it's the local gendarme and he's checking me out. Damn!

I take this all in and immediately look away hoping to blend into the scenery. Good luck.

There's twelve feet of bar between me and the guy at the end and a couple of tables to choose from, but where does 'Stalin' pick to drink? You guessed it. He lumbers up to within two feet of me, on my right side, sets his gun on the bar between us and orders a Slivovitz. As he throws it back, I steal a look at the gun. I can't believe it. A US made Thompson sub-machine gun like you see in the old gangster movies, only this one has a straight clip, not the barrel clip like ya saw Al Capone use. I'm thinking 'This would draw a good price in the States.'

He orders another drink, turns my way and looks me up and down with his piercing brown eyes, taking it all in. What conclusion he comes to isn't positive by the look in his eyes when ours meet. I smile, he doesn't. I take another quick glance at his gun. There's a hair-line crack in the wooden forearm and the selector switch is on "fully automatic." Damn! What kind of day to day trouble does he face?

I want to ask to see his gun, but not even the Slivovitz can suppress the 'vibes' I'm picking up from this guy. This is Tito's Yugoslavia; time to get the hell out of here! I throw back my shot and head for the door. I hear the volks pull up as I walk out. Graham and Steve want to drink to the success of fixing the car. I say "No, No, not here. I'll explain later as I jump in the car and we head off.

38. The Coastal Road

Graham and Steve had come down the 'central corridor' of Yugoslavia to get to Greece as I had. So we decided to circle around Albania and take the coast road along the Adriatic.

I thought Tito had a lid on Yugoslavia? It was nothing compared to the tyranny in Albania. I never met anyone with a story about traveling through Albania. It wasn't even possible to get a transit visa.

The coast was magnificent. The view of the sea and the bluffs over-looking it was stunning. Their beauty was in complete contrast to the road itself. Truly the worst road I've ever encountered that I had to go any real distance on.

If the entire US Airforce 'saturation' bombed it, there couldn't have been another pot-hole. It was like a slice of Swiss cheese, only they would have culled this slice because it was all holes, only air and no cheese. The pot-holes were all six to eight inches deep; their size varied, but there was never more than two feet between them. Ten miles per hour was about maximum speed, and then we'd be thrown from side to side.

Riding in the back seat, bumping my head on the roof and not being able to enjoy the scenery was driving me nuts. About six hours of that and we called it quits.

I noticed some caves in the bluffs and thought maybe they would be a good place to sleep. We hauled our sleeping bags up to one and settled in for the night. We heard a car pull up down below, doors opening and people climbing up the slope. Sure enough, it was the police. Not

'Stalin' with his sub-machine gun, thank God. He was probably still back at the bar. These guys looked like 'highway patrol'.

I knew Graham could speak some German and a lot of Yugoslavs could too.

"Don't try to talk with these guys; let's act like stupid tourists that can't understand anything." I said.

It worked. They were obviously telling us we couldn't stay here, but gave up in frustration. I bet they laughed and joked later how stupid we were. So what, at least we had a place to stay.

The next morning, looking out from the cave on the side of the bluff, on the Adriatic and her islands was breathtaking. Until I looked straight down and saw that damn road, still full of holes. It took a lot of the joy away.

The beer was gone, but I still had some hash left to ease the pain. We came onto a construction gang around noon working on the road. I laughed and said "What do you think they're repairing?"

I stopped laughing when I saw the answer. A rock slide completely covered the road from the bluff to the sea. No way around. We were told we'd have to drive sixty miles back to get the detour around the slide. I flipped out.

Already three hours of hell on this road today and now we have to go back the way we came. That thought pushed me over the edge.

I started yelling and waving my arms around, cursing and swearing saying 'where was the sign telling us to take the detour? There was no fucking sign! Go put a fucking sign back there so people know! What's the matter with you guys? 'Son of a bitch.'

They all stopped working and looked at me like I was nuts. A couple of them said something to each other and pointed at me, but nobody laughed. Good thing.

We turned the car around. I said "Let me Drive."

I had a theory which I rationally explained: Maybe, by going sixty or seventy mph, we could skip over the potholes and touch down on the flat two foot areas in-between. Graham and Steve weren't so sure but by the look on my face they thought we'd better give it a try. I figured we'd just keep accelerating until we hit that smooth spot and maintain that speed. Trouble was, we never hit it. I'm sure the theory was right, but the old volks couldn't go fast enough, not that we didn't try. What a ride! Must have been a sight, because everyone we saw, stopped what they were doing and watched us.

We made it like that for about twenty miles before the first blow-out. We all got out to change the tire and did a walk around the car. All the hub caps were gone and the wheels were bent as if somebody took a ten pound sledge hammer to them. I never saw such a thing. It was a wonder they held air at all. I cracked up, and the guys joined in.

There's a certain level of insanity, when reached, opens a release valve on your frustration, by destroying our little car, we reached it. Feeling better, with a tinge of guilt, we changed the tire and having no more spares, we were back in the ten mph hell again.

The little volks never quite ran the same after that. However, the exercise did attest to the durability of the 'people's car'.

We finished off the Dalmatian coast and crossed into Italy at Trieste. Seemed as though Yugoslavia was a challenge; once faced and passed, it was all down hill to Paris.

Neither the Italians, the Swiss, nor the French caught the discrepancy in the papers for the car. Every border we came to, the guards would look the car over, see the wheels and just shake their heads. The Swiss guy actually bent down, grabbed the wheel and started shaking it to see if it was loose I said "hey Hey HEY easy there, we've got to get this thing to Paris." He gave me a dirty look, but didn't say anything. I'll bet it must have been wobbling as we drove up.

39. Summertime in Paris

I got off in Paris. The boys were heading home to England. They ended up owing me about forty bucks US for food and miscellaneous. We exchanged addresses and I said I'd be over in a couple of weeks to visit.

I found out later, the English customs caught them for trying to import the volks into England without paying the tax on the car. We had come all that way and it was the English that smelled 'the rat'. It cost the boys about $125.

That was the only border I didn't cross with that car. As far as I know it never crossed another. Because when I arrived in Worthing, in southern England where the boys lived; Graham told me he wrecked it while celebrating their home coming. Too bad, so sad.

Paris in the summer,--it was beautiful! Walking along the river Seine with the barges tied to the walls and all the bridges, each with an architectural statement of its own, lent an air of timelessness one could easily get lost in. The smell of the water, fresh baked bread, the restaurants, and oh yes, the smell of cattle; no, that was the herd of people I was in the middle of; walking up the street.

The buildings weren't more than five stories high giving the city a warmer, lived in feeling. The museums,--the art and culture—one would need months, if not years to digest. Who has that? So you have to see and experience what you can in the time you have and look forward to the next visit.

That was exactly my plan. I didn't think I'd stay long. My experience with the people in the shops, bars and cafés was disappointing. Not speaking French put me at an extreme disadvantage. If you don't at least start in French, they become arrogant, impatient and down right rude. I certainly wasn't fashion conscious and quite accurately looked like I had no money and no place to stay. That wasn't exactly endearing me with the shop keepers.

The number system was difficult. When buying something and asking "how much?" it was impossible to understand what they said. Imagine: the number ninety-eight is said "four times twenty plus eighteen." Give me a Break!!

They would peak into my hand to see how much money was there and more than once, you can believe, they just scrapped my hand clean of the coins and said "c'est assey"---that's enough! Being short of money and prospects, my temper flared a lot, almost coming to blows with the 'garcons.'

> ** I found the French rude and insulting until I returned years later after living in Quebec and having knowledge of the language. Even speaking what I would call a 'back woods lumberjack French with no front teeth,' the people in France were very helpful and friendly.*

~~~

I always gravitated toward the universities where there were stimulating conversations and interesting people, to say nothing of cheap food. I was looking at a list of classes and dreaming about taking one. Then I could say "While studying at the Sorbonne in Paris I -----blah blah blah." It beats the hell out of-- "While in Paris, I was sleeping in the parks or under a bridge---blah blah." That's when Linda bumped into me with her tray of food and brought me out of my dream world.

Linda was from England; taking her last semester before graduating with a degree in French literature. She was tall by French standards, with long curly hair, a round face and a beautiful smile. Her auburn hair was streaked with a multitude of natural colors that radiated off the sunlight coming in from the windows.

She apologized in French, I responded in English. "Oh, a Yank?" she smiled. "And what brings you here? She asked, as I walked her over to a table where we sat down.

"My education" I said, which was partially true, though a bit misleading. There was an immediate and strong attraction for each other. Her serious, goal orientated, studious attributes conflicted somewhat with my 'laisser-faire' attitude, but when she told me about her place in the Latin Quarter, I knew I could overcome any obstacle in the relationship.

While she studied during the day, I would be sight seeing and during the evening she would show me the nightlife of Paris from a student's perspective. These were good days; carefree and happy, especially after coming back from the failed attempt at 'cars and the black market in Turkey.'

The Latin Quarter was a source of turmoil and unrest in 69 and 70. There had recently been violent, destructive riots in the streets, mostly led by students. On every major intersection or within sight of each other was a blue school bus full of military police. I noticed some guys had wings on their uniforms which meant they were Air-borne paratroopers; France's elite fighting units, keeping a constant vigilance on the crowds.

"What's this about?" I wondered. I had heard about the police in Paris, but—Damn---These guys wouldn't take any crap from anybody. They hassled young travelers, especially those that were living on the 'margins.' Lots of stories floated around about police stopping you to check your papers and if you didn't happen to have them on you they threw you in jail until they got around to finding out who you were. That might be this week or next. I had a nightmare about it.

40. The Riot

There was unrest brewing constantly under the surface and one night it raised its ugly head. Being on the street a lot I should have seen it coming, but I didn't have a finger on the pulse. I was doing my 'tourist' thing; drinking in the art and architecture with guzzling intemperance and getting all the news I needed on the weather report. Since I had a place to stay, I didn't care about much else.

This is how it happened. I was drinking wine in a down and dirty, basement café not far from Linda's place with a bunch of students. We were having a good conversation when the atmosphere changed in a heart beat; from cool and calm to fear approaching panic.

The owner starts throwing us all out waving his arms and yelling something I didn't understand. I was one of the last to leave, seeing how I had to finish that thirty cent glass of wine. One word kept trumping all the others---emeute—emeute—RIOT!

As I walked out, the owner gave me a shove and pulled down the metal shutter on his shop, closed and locked the door.

The smell of tear gas set my nostrils on fire. There was chaos in the street. To my left was a solid line of military police armed with helmets, clubs and shields moving down the street in a wide sweep heading my way. Behind the main line was a lot more police in smaller groups.

I ducked into a doorway and watched the main line pass. They looked at me with some disdain but didn't do anything to break formation.

Then a cop from a small group saw me, reached out, grabbed me out of the doorway and threw me into the street where I stumbled into another cop. He turned and hit me with his club on my shoulder. I spun around and fell against another cop and he smacked me too. I started speaking English real loud so they knew I was a foreigner but it didn't seem to help. They pushed me through the main line, but before I got through they got two more licks in. These weren't love taps; I was hurting and scared!

Now I was out in front and hauled ass down the street away from the army turning at the first intersection only to come face to face with a street FULL of students armed with rocks, bottles and clubs. Fired up and ready for action; I saw a few cock back their arms to throw so I yelled and waved my arms "Whoa, Whoa, Stop—Stop.

They lowered their arms. I told them the army is right behind me, right there---pointing at the corner frantically.

Getting caught between them and the police line was certain death. I pushed my way though the crowd and started running, flat out, for two more blocks and leaned against a light post to catch my breath. My heart was pounding so hard I thought it was going to beat its way right out of my chest.

There was a surreal serenity, under that light post. Everyone that wasn't participating in the riot down the street was home, locked up tight with the shades drawn.

Get this: I'm catching my breath, the street is deserted, except for one guy and he's walking toward me. As he gets under the light, I recognize him. My God, it's Frank. I can't believe it. I'm over whelmed.

"George, what are you doing here"? He says.

I tell him I just got my ass kicked by the cops and was in the middle of the riot down the street. "No shit? He asks

"Yeah, no shit! Listen" We can hear glass breaking, screams and the thud of clubs on shields. Frank's watching me while we're listening and says "You're bleeding."

A drop of blood was hanging from my ear. One of the night sticks that hit me put a little split in my scalp above my ear and it was staining my shirt. I'm thinking 'damn, I don't need this; I've only got two shirts to my name' when Frank breaks my train of thought by asking "Where are you staying?"

"With an English girl not far from here,---but I don't think I can get there from here and live to tell about it."

He said his place was around the corner and to come stay with him.

I was never so glad to see anyone as I was to see Frank right then. He had an attic atelier. One room looking out on the roof tops of Paris. It was a most welcome refuge, quiet, safe and off the streets of chaos and anarchy that were so pleasant earlier in the day.

The experience must have sucked a lot of energy out of me because I slept like a 'rock' until noon the next day.

We woke up and had breakfast in a café down stairs. I hit the 'replay' button in my mind and went over it all with Frank again. It all seemed so surreal. Like a dream that never happened except for the proof of the bruises from the night sticks of the cops.

Frank knew Paris better than I did and he thought I was lucky not to have been beaten up worse and woken up in jail, instead of his place.

The more I thought about it; the way I met Frank under that street light with nobody else around; and him giving me refuge like he did---That ain't luck!!!

~~~~

Over croissants and café au laits, Frank told me how his French was progressing and his plans to return to Montreal in a couple of months. I told him I would be there one day, so he gave me the address of his parents figuring they'd know how to reach him.

Sure enough! A few years later I was in Montreal and looked him up. He had a Dutch girlfriend who was the sister of a friend of mine back in Utrecht Holland. Small world!!

We said our 'good byes' and I headed back to Linda's place. Thought letting her lick my wounds and nursing me back to health was a good idea. And it was, but the shine on the image of Paris had a bit of a scuffing to it.

We stayed together a couple more days and then I left for England to find Steve and Graham. The boys owed me a few 'bucks' from the trip up north and I needed to collect. It was sad leaving Linda, but we both knew the fun was wearing off and it was time for me to hit the road.

I left in the morning, hitch-hiking to Calais on the coast of France to catch the ferry to England. There was a new method to cross the channel, a hovercraft 'riding on air' so to speak. Cost a couple of bucks more, but what the heck, I should be picking up a few bucks from the boys when we meet.

Did I say "Riding on air?" Hardly! The wind was up and there was a chop on the water. That old familiar smell started permeating the air by the time we were half way across. It didn't seem like that rough of a ride, but there was a bunch of people hanging over the rail, tossing their cookies. I think everybody was glad to finally see those white cliffs of Dover come into view.

41. English and England

After she was all tied up tight to the dock; I disembarked onto another new country. This time, with a feeling of confidence and exhilaration, knowing I could speak with everyone here. This was England and we're all speaking English right? I'd written off the linguistic challenges I had with Ronnie, thinking he was a bit strange anyway.

To prove the point, I walked up to the first guy I could. He was wearing blue cover- alls and up to his waist in a hole he was digging in the street. I asked him where the bus terminal was. Good thing I already knew, because by the time he was done talking, pointing and waving I realized I only understood about half of what he said. Damn! How could this be? My exhilaration was deflating fast and turning into anger.

It got worse! I went to the bus terminal to get a ticket out of town so I could hitch-hike south to Worthing where Steve and Graham live.

The cahier says "That'll be to 'bob' dearie." What the hell's a "bob"? I'm thinking. When the guy behind me says "Two 'quid' mate."

Might as well be in France, because I'm back to holding out my hand for them to take what I owe. And it ain't over yet! The guy behind me kindly explains to this 'stupid yank' that England is not on the decimal system. There's twelve cents to a shilling, twelve shillings to a pound, or is that a quid, or a bob?

There for awhile, I thought I was either over paying by two or being cheated by two. And the merchant or barkeep thought I was trying to short them. Add a couple of beers to the equation and there's lots of potential for drama. Thank God for the honesty of the English people.

There was no bluffing them either. They'd fight at the drop of a hat. I was in my first pub paying for a beer and I didn't give the barkeep enough money. I was still in that decimal mode, ten cents to a dime thing. It started to go bad. He thought I was cheating him and I was sure I paid enough, besides; I could hardly understand what he was saying. Then it was off with his apron and around the bar he comes when a patron I'd been talking to says "Hey, he's a yank, he doesn't know any better."

We went through it all again and I finally got it. The atmosphere turned back to congeniality. Paid the right amount, walked out the door, crossed the street and waited for the next car heading south.

Here it comes. What?!! Yep, I'm on the wrong side of the street. Damn! I don't know how many times I stepped off a curb to hear squealing brakes and see obscene gestures from motorists. It's a wonder I didn't get killed that first week.

42. You Yanks

I was dropped off in Hastings. Hastings! Can you imagine the history? I had a sixth grade teacher with a name like a bug; He put his chair on his desk, climbed on the desk and stood on his chair with his head almost touching the ceiling and said "1066—1066' This is the only year England was ever invaded and conquered. If you miss this question on the test I will flunk you for the year."

The invasion took place at Hastings and now I was here. Wasn't much of a town, but it still called for a celebration. I could at least toast that teacher.

Into the first pub I saw. "Pint of double D please," and I knew what to pay. That's progress! I had two more and was starting to talk louder and laugh longer. There was a descent afternoon crowd and I had the attention of a few guys with some story when I made an off the cuff remark about the queen. Now, I kid you not. The earth stood still. You could hear a pin drop inside, even with the flow of traffic outside. Two guys stood up at the next table with menacing looks. They weren't leaving, they were coming for me.

The guys I was talking with when I dropped 'the bomb' intercepted them, pleading ignorance on my behalf. After all, I was just a stupid Yank! I agreed whole-heartedly. They set about instructing me that any off-color remark about the queen or the royal family might pass in some places, but not here. And if I ever wanted to start trouble, just start running down the queen and somebody would oblige me.

I used discretion from that time on. It was always 'open season' on the government, but not the queen or any of the 'Royals'.

A little later, in the same pub, I met an old man---a very old man who came up to me and said "We could have taken you anytime." He lost me, but right then, that wouldn't have been that hard.

"Yeah, we could have beaten you easily." He said He must have seen the puzzled look on my face, so he points at my chest and says "Your revolutionary war. We could have beaten you."

"Yeah, I'm sure you could have. I just don't understand why you didn't?"

Well, that soured the water a bit. But damn, I couldn't tell you the last time I thought about the Revolutionary War. That includes a lot of 4th of July celebrations! Our two hundredth anniversary was coming up and this old boy must have been taking it to heart. Some people just can't let go.

In fact, it was the next day. Hitch-hiking wasn't going to well, so I took a bus the rest of the way to Worthing. I got on and sat next to another old man. He was thin, with white hair, wire rimmed glasses and a blue sport coat. A 'gentlemen.' We start talking and he says "You're a Yank, aren't you?"

"Yes sir."

"You know, you didn't win back then."

Pause---I'm thinking 'weren't we together on that? WWII and WWI? He sees the puzzled look and says "Your war of independence."

I start laughing, thinking about the day before.

He says "It was all Cornwallis---a lack of communication."

"You're quite right." "Would you accept Richard Nixon as a compensatory gift?"

He starts laughing and we talk about lighter things the rest of the trip.

It was amazing. Ya know, traveling really is the best form of education.

43. The Southern Coast

I arrived in Worthing, late in the afternoon. It was another beautiful summer day. Worthing is a laid back little sea coast town in the south of England. A lot of old people retire down there and sit by the beach and look out to sea. There was a belief that the seaweed which washed up on the beach had some health benefit, increased longevity, apparently.

I was walking behind an old couple when one says to the other "Didn't we sit over there yesterday?" "Let's sit here today." I noticed the newspapers left on the benches were opened to the obituaries. Damn, I thought. If this is what there is to look forward too---then to hell with longevity; I'm living for today! And I did!

I looked Graham up first. He was living with his parents in their story and a half brick house with a tile roof. It was a nice place. Windows let a lot of light in and even though it wasn't right on the coast, you could smell the fresh sea air. They had a spare bedroom I could stay in.

We caught up with Steve that evening. They showed me the night life in Brighton and their favorite pubs along the coast.

We were tossing back a few beers in one pub when the clock struck 5:00PM. "Last call." The barkeep calls out.

"What's this?" I asked.

They said it was the law. The government had to make a law to close the pubs between five and seven or nobody would go home for dinner. The cartoon figure 'Andy Capp' came to mind. I could understand it. English beer is different from anything I'd had on the continent. It's brown, little to no carbonation and tastes watery on the first try. But once one acquires a taste for it, there's nothing else that will satisfy.

I acquired the taste---and then some! I loved it. If somebody would have cut me, I'd have probably bled brown. Since the alcohol is sucking the moisture out of your body and the beer is thin, watery and extremely tasty. One tries to quench a thirst that is really quite unquenchable; which makes for a remarkable evening, but a little rough the next day. The cure: Have another at ten AM when the pubs open.

The weekend came and there were a couple of parties the boys wanted to go to. We left the pub around eleven to go to the first. It was interesting. Everybody was hammered. Graham and Steve were riding high on their recent exploits, telling big tales of their trip to Greece and Yugoslavia to the girls. I was the verifiable proof.

We were leaving the first party for the next when Steve said "Why don't you drive George?" I guess I didn't appear as loaded as they were----or they didn't want to get a 'DWI.'

"Ya sure,why not" I got behind the wheel, pulled out of the driveway, looked left of course, and almost got plowed into from a guy coming from the right----of course! There's those squealing brakes and skidding tire sounds again.

They drive pretty well here, or else we'd have been nailed but good. We yelled back and forth at the guy, and then at each other, coming to the conclusion---that guy just couldn't take a joke. It was a little Austin Mini we were in and I killed it in all the commotion. Fired it back up and headed down the road to the next party----on the wrong side of the road.

"Pull over George, I think I'd better drive" says Graham.

And that's where this part of the story ends, because I can't remember the next party or the rest of the night!!

44. George the V

The next day we all went swimming in the Sea, where the old people congregate to smell the rotting sea weed so they can live a little longer. There wasn't a cloud in the sky and the temperature was about 85 degrees. The water was cold, clear and refreshing, especially after last nights 'boozer'. It felt like the Sea was washing the poison from the night before off my body through each and every pore in my skin.

It was medicinal, a body message; my mind was in a transcendent mode toward a higher plain with no outside chemical stimulus, when Graham yells "Look out! Clear the way. There's a George the V".

"What?"

"A George the V, right there!"

I'm brought down from Nirvana to be shown a big human turd---a brown trout so to speak, floating lazily by.

"Son of a b___!!! You could have gone all day without showing me that!" I said.

"What did you call that?"

"Never mind, I don't want to hear the details."

The scene itself said enough. Obviously the people didn't hold their former monarch George V up for admiration.

~~~

During the next couple of days, I got Graham and Steve to cough-up better than half the money they owed me from the trip up from Greece. They thought I should pay some of the duty they had to pay when they got caught bringing the volks into England. Didn't seem logical to me, but it was obvious I wasn't going to get any more money out of them.

My welcome was wearing thin and I'd seen the sights. Amsterdam and Hamburg were calling, where the girls were prettier and 'easier' to talk too. So, it was good bye to the boys and off toward Holland.

45. Back in Amsterdam

I caught a train to Harwich and took the boat to the Hoek Van Holland. Blowing right through London without stopping weighed heavily on me, but I knew I would be back one day.

Passed through Dutch customs easy enough and hitchhiked up to Amsterdam where I stayed with Eric again. Saw Quint and a few other friends I'd made when I was here last. They all wanted to know how the "Turkey" trip went and if I'd made it as far as Nepal like I'd planned. I told them the story a few times. About getting caught at the border and being turned back into Greece.

They all thought I was lucky not to be rotting in some Turkish jail. I remember Frank saying the same thing about a French jail. It made me appreciate my freedom.

Went to all the familiar places; partying hard, day and night. I was frequenting the places the locals went, where there were few to no tourists and starting, just starting to feel at home. Certainly no 'native' by any stretch, but blending in just the same.

There was "Olde Man Jap's" café, just around the corner and down a side street from Damm square. A nondescript shop front, but when entering, you had to wave your hand to cut the hashish smoke to find a place to sit down and order a coffee. There was always 'big smoke' and 'big business' going on.

Transactions of large quantities were happening under the surface with only small deals changing hands in view.

Usually some samples of the 'quantity' or somebody's 'best' which just arrived in town.

The old man was stoop-shouldered with wire rimmed glasses, thinning white hair and appeared to be a bit feeble as he brought you a coffee, but that was not the case. He ran a 'tight ship'. A number of times I saw him fly around the counter, throw off his apron and grab some guy by the back of the neck and throw him out the door---never to be allowed back in. It was always some shady, deviant, villainess type that looked like they'd just crawled out from under a rock; never the smokers or straight –up dealers of good report.

It took years to be accepted, or at least acknowledged by the clientele. In all that time the 'old man' was always good to me.

There were restaurants and bars where you could eat and drink cheap. Where Dutch musicians would play Dixieland or the blues like you heard in New Orleans, but with no tourists. It took time to find these places and they weren't listed in "Europe On $5.00 a Day". But I'm getting ahead of myself. That's for the sequel.

46. Because I Like to get High

Don't think for a moment that 'soft drugs' like hashish and marijuana were legal. They weren't. The police would bust you in a heart beat if they thought you were a dealer or smuggler, while choosing to turn a 'blind-eye' on the users.

One day in Vondel Park, in the center of Amsterdam, where it was common for young people to congregate and catch a 'buzz,' while old retirees fished in the ponds hoping to catch big, dirty, brown carp; I was sitting on a bench watching the fisherman while a friend named Jan sat next to me rolling a joint. He had long wavy brown hair down to his shoulders, a loose-fitting long sleeve white India cotton shirt and a green Syrian vest with beads and little mirrors sown onto it.

He was immersed in his project, with all the makings on his lap, as two Policeman drove right up to us in a little Volkswagen and rolled down their window. I never heard or saw them coming. If they'd have been six inches closer, they would have run-over our feet.

The driver says through his open window "What are you doing there?"

I shut-up and pretend I'm invisible. I know Jan is 'lit' from the last joint.

He answers "I'm rolling a joint."

Now this is no single paper joint. It's three papers with a cardboard filter.

"Why?" asks the cop.

"Because it's a beautiful day and I want to get stoned and enjoy it."

The cop looks at his partner, shakes his head and drives off. I go from visions of jail, to ecstasy, not believing what just happened. Course, that's the same kind of interaction I would have had with the police in St. Louis, in the same situation. Yeah, right!! More like this: "Up against the wall M.F., feet back, spread your legs apart and don't move. You're going to jail!"

Don't ya just love those cultural differences? Does one seem more civilized than another?

47. Father Knew Best

I needed to get my head straight, see some scenery and get some fresh air into my lungs. Heading out on the highway, hitch-hiking to Hamburg seemed to be the best answer.

It took six hours to hitch-hike four hundred miles. Who needs a car? That's faster than the train!

Another beautiful day, with sunshine, blue skies and a few white puffy clouds drifting by as I stood by the highway waiting for a ride. The new growth forests of spruce trees all planted in straight lines filled the air with the scent of Christmas wreathes. Times like these you don't care if you get a ride or not.

A farmer picked me up. I could smell the stable on his clothes and the manure on his shoes. He dropped me off at a rural exit on the Autobahn not far from Bremen. There was about twenty head of black and white Holstein milk cows lying down in the field along the highway.

When I was child, my father taught me how to call cows in German. He grew up on a farm in Illinois speaking German at home. My grandfather came over when he was seventeen.

I saw those cows lying down and thought "What the heck, I'll give it a try."

Cupped my hands, put them to my mouth and hollered what sounded like "sook sook sook."

Damned if they didn't all stand up and walk over to the fence! Couldn't help but laugh as I walked down and scratched them on the forehead and behind the ears. He would have been proud of me. I wondered then, if the other things he tried to teach me were true too. Hmmm.

48. HH

I got into Hamburg in the late afternoon and went to the University to hang-out. Had dinner there and then ran into Dieter Rink. Not wanting to hear the 'party line' just then I went to Frank's bar in search of Volker, pronounced FALLKA.

Frank said Volker was out of town, probably back home in Heidelberg for a few days. I had a couple of beers there, and then went to "Charlie's" place to smoke a little with the boys. It was getting on ten PM. I kept thinking about Volker's girlfriend, Nadia. He had introduced us the first time I was in Hamburg. I walked over to her place. Mistake #1. She let me in. Mistake #2.

Nadia had blue eyes and blonde hair. She stood all of six feet tall, a big girl, but not an ounce of fat on her. She was awkward in the kitchen, always knocking over or dropping something but in the matters of love, she was agile, adept and proficient.

Nadia taught history at the high school level. Being a 'card carrying' communist party member, it was illegal for her to hold a teaching job in Germany. No communists or Nazis allowed.

She had a small one bedroom efficiency on the second floor of a post war apartment building. When I came over she wanted to talk of the 'wonders' of communism. I had more basic thoughts, me man—you woman, let's do it. We compromised and did both.

I stayed with her for three days. Volker called on the third day. I didn't talk to him. Nadia cried a little when she hung up. She told him I was there. Great! A George the V I am-I am. It was never the same between Volker and me.

It was a very foolish thing to have done and yet after realizing this, it was less than six months later that I would do it again. "Like a dog returns to its' vomit."

You might say "let reason will out" but a man can reason anything out—and justify it. More truthful and accurate would be Proverbs 16:25 "There's a way that seems right unto a man, but the end thereof is death." It was certainly the death of a friendship more valuable than a fleeting moment of pleasure.

Nadia walked me to the U-bahn station. She was off to teach school and I – I was just off. I never saw her again and didn't hear if she was prosecuted for being a communist or if she was fired from her job. No Communists or Nazis allowed.

49. Love on the Lake

Melancholy best describes the next couple of days in Hamburg. Overcast, dull and rainy, but then the sun came out and people were lying on the grass around the Binnen Alster.

The Alster is a large lake in the center of Hamburg divided into two by the Lombard Bridge. I was walking along the Binnen or inside Alster which has a couple of major hotels, the American Consulate and a row of seventeenth century warehouses with copper roofs and beautiful gabled ends facing the lake. During the war it was said, they tore the copper off the roofs and used it for munitions, but it was back on in 1970.

It was well after noon as I went into a pastry shop to have a coffee and sweet cake. I made my selection and went outside to sit at a table in the sunshine. The sweet cakes in Europe were incredible; each country having their own specialty. I think I've already gone into that. But right now I was looking at the 'sweet cake' sitting at the table next to me with her girlfriend and I was salivating!

She was looking at me and knew I was a foreigner. I asked for the sugar just to speak too her and she replied with an English accent.

Biergida was 5'6" with green eyes and long beautiful auburn hair; the kind that radiates multitudes of colors when the sun shines on it.

The girls had been shopping on the Monkeburg Strasse, a walking street full of shops and boutiques and now wanted to take a stroll along the Aster. I asked if I could join them and they said yes. We all finished our coffee and cakes and got up to leave. Biergida said something to her girlfriend and handed over her packages to her and she turned and left; leaving Biergida and me to walk together.

We made small talk while watching the ducks and swans swim. She told me she was a student but didn't know yet what she would major in. I thought it wouldn't matter; this girl could make it on her looks alone.

She pulled a plastic bag from her purse with bread in it and started feeding the ducks. Soon we were inundated with them. Laughing and joking about the ducks showed her smile to be bright and cheerful with full lips and straight teeth. Her laugh, exposed the young and carefree souls we both were.

I told her of the places I'd been and some of the things I'd done. And soon I'd be going to Denmark.

She asked "Where are you staying?"

"I have no place" which was true. Laughingly I asked "Could I come home with you?"

She looked me in the eye and smiled. We looked deep into each other for a moment.

Then she said "Yes, you can."

I reached out and held her by the shoulders and kissed her. A beautiful, telling moment.

She gave me her address and said she still lived at home; to come after ten o'clock when her parents would be sleeping and leave before they got up in the morning. I almost fell into the lake! I thought—if you dropped a rope from the 5th floor I'd be there.

We walked on for awhile just enjoying the beauty of the day. She had to be getting back home soon so we parted with a kiss and the promise of meeting later on.

Seemed like it took forever for the clock to roll around to ten, but it did and at 10:15 I gave a light tap on her door. She answered in a long flowing night gown that seemed to shimmer in the dark, while at the same time accenting the beauty of her young figure. She took my hand and led me through her parent's apartment to the back where her room was.

It was a post war building like most buildings were in Hamburg. The hardwood floors creaked and groaned as we made our way to her room. My heart leapt in fear with every little noise that her parents would wake up. I knew I had to wake up and get out before they did, which didn't lend to a deep restful sleep.

We had a wonderful beautiful night together. As we paused between our acts of passion to let our bodies re-charge, she told me she was seventeen. It clicked then why she hadn't picked a major to study---she was still in high school. I might have been a year and a half ahead of her in age, but not in the art of pleasure.

I woke up in time, crept out of her parents place just as I heard stirring in their room. Biergida had to attend classes so we agreed to do the same thing the next night.

Was it worth it? Yes, oh yes, but was it really? I lay there wondering what the gun laws were in Germany. If this happened in St. Louis, her father could blow my brains out and never spend a day in jail. Picturing my grey brain matter splattered over the back wall of her bedroom because I overslept, definitely took the edge off of any future rendezvous. Two nights were enough. It wasn't the loving-- it was the worrying. I told her I was going to Denmark tomorrow. She cried.

50. Thumbs out for Scandinavia

I was up early the next day, that's for sure! Out on the Autobahn, hitch-hiking north through Lubeck to Puttgarden. That was the northern most point to catch the ferry to Rodby Havn in Denmark, then on to Copenhagen.

It was an overcast day and rain was imminent. I don't know if it was the weather or the thought of leaving Biergida that was making me gloomy. But it was obviously time to move on. A little sunshine and blue skies would do wonders but that wasn't going to happen. The clouds were thick and ominous and I knew I was going to get wet.

I can't believe it. A black Mercedes sport coup pulls over to give me a ride. I open the door to see black leather seats and a mid thirty's guy with short cropped hair motioning me to get in. He's got leather driving gloves on, holding the wheel he starts twisting his wrists to get a better grip when he says "Are you ready?"

Ready? Hell yes I'm ready and with that I nod my head. Immediately my neck snaps back and my head hits the headrest as we burn through all the gears and level off doing 250 km per hour. That's about 150mph. The scenery is flying by until we drive into a torrential down pour and he backs it down to 80 mph. It seems like we're doing 30. The rain lets up and back up to 150 we go. The guy has a death grip on the wheel. Good thing, because one slight slip and we'd be toast. You never see an ambulance in a big hurry going to an accident on the

Autobahn. They must all be fatal. It's pretty easy to see why, but God, what a rush.

We arrive in Lubeck in good time, would have been record time if not for the rain. I'm glad to get out because this guy is playing like he's in the Indy 500. He pulls over and I get out and thank him. As soon as I close the door, he burns off and I can hear him shifting gears, a few seconds later he's out of sight and I'm wondering if it all really happened. It did, because I'm here in Lubeck.

The clouds are building back up and it's about to pour again when a little volks stops for me. Just like the one I tried to sell in Turkey. He gives me a ride up to Oldenburg at 60 mph. Oh well, back to reality. That's fine; at least I'm out of the rain. As I get out, it stops raining. Tis a charmed life I'm leading and I don't want it to stop now.

It's still twenty-five miles to Puttgarden where the ferry is and a little more challenging to get a ride. It's a small road and the people going this way are most likely taking the ferry. Now that would seem to be to my advantage, but it's not.

People are generally leery about taking strangers across a border. If I were to be searched and found to be carrying something illegal, it would be a hassle and time consuming for them. And I must say I look the part.

Finally a young Danish couple with a baby takes the chance. They are returning from holidays in Switzerland on Lago de Lugano. They'll drop me off at the ferry where I'll pass through customs by myself. Then meet back up with them on the boat and ride with them up to Copenhagen. Perfect.

51. Copenhagen

It worked like a charm. I passed through customs easy enough, jumped back on with them and rode the rest of the way to Copenhagen. They dropped me off in front of the Tivoli Gardens, a fantastic amusement park and meticulously manicured garden.

I went through the free part but wasn't going to spend any money on rides seeing how my funds were diminishing quickly. The gardens were world renowned but to me they looked like a good place to sleep if I couldn't do better. And I figured I would, especially after cruising the streets and seeing all the young people in the parks and in the city squares. I couldn't believe how open and friendly they were. So willing to talk and listen and to meet new people and hear about different far–off places.

That in itself was astounding. But what really caught my eye and was hard to believe was the GIRLS. There were more of them than there were guys first off. Second the majority were beautiful. Not just cute---but stunningly so. I guess since there were so many of them they didn't have such a 'big head' like they do in the States. They were approachable.

It got to be like a game for me. I'd wait and watch to see the most beautiful one walk by, stop her and start talking. I'd ask something like "what should I see here or what shouldn't I miss in Copenhagen?" More often than not they'd start telling me about their favorite places and what not to miss and even take me there. If things were really going well, I'd tell them I had no place to stay and more than once they asked me to come home with them. I love Denmark. Actually all of North Europe opened up to me. I never once paid a hotel in Germany, Holland or Denmark,---a couple of Youth Hostels and a few flop houses, but no hotels.

52. The Danes

I met Liese and Anja in a park called Orsteds in the center of Copenhagen. They were on a walking bridge, leaning on the rail looking into the water.

Liese had long thick red hair, about 5'10" with a long face and pale white skin that accented her little turned up nose and bright blue eyes. I have fair skin as well and I never got a tan. My summers went in stages of white to red to peal and back to white to start all over again. Liese was in that stage from white to red. My heart went out to her. She looked great. Me---I never did.

Anja was a few inches shorter than Liese. She had the Nordic blue eyes and long brown hair streaked with sun shades, a deep rich olive tan that cried out to be touched and an inviting smile with full natural red lips.

I made my approach, "beautiful day, girls."

They turned, looked at me and smiled. Anja says "you're English."

Liese, "American."

I point at Liese and say "you got it."

Liese gives Anja a nudge, that all knowing, international posture—'see, I'm right.'

We laugh and start talking about the park, Copenhagen, what's happening in town. They say something to each other in Danish, turn to me and ask "we're going for a coffee and a pastry. Do you want to come along?"

Let's see---beautiful girls, coffee and pastries---Hell yes! "Ya sure" I said. "I've been making a study of pastries all over Europe. You must tell me about the Danish ones."

We made our way across the bridge and along the edge of the lake heading for the nearest pastry shop, which was never very far away in Copenhagen. They told me about the almond paste and different flavors as we approached a clump of grass and some bushes at the edge of the lake.

All of sudden a huge black swan stands on it legs, spreads its' wings to their full span, starts beating them and hissing at us. I jump in front of Liese and Anja pushing them back and away from the swan. Once at a safe distance they started laughing and pointing at two little babies the swan was protecting.

Anja says "That was brave, George."

"Yes it was." Says Liese

I just laughed. Truth be told that damn swan scared the shit out of me. And I wasn't done with her yet. I'd never seen anything like that before. I approached it again. It did the same thing, standing up with full wings expanded, hissing and coming at me. The thing stood all of five feet tall and was menacing to say the least,----formidable really.

I could see why Ludwig at Neuschwanstein, (the Disney castle) picked a swan to be on his coat of arms. They're bad!!!

The girls didn't like me teasing the swan, but heck, I figured it was part of my education.

We took off from there toward our original destination---pastries! We had our coffee and I sampled a number of delicious Danish treats. The girls wanted to show me their part of town. It was South of Gothersgade, the main street that cut the city in half. It's a beautiful area full of old buildings standing alongside their modern counterparts, a collage of scenic architecture full of beautiful people.

I learned where the best sweet cake shops were and the vending machines they used at night to sell the pastries they hadn't sold in the day. They showed me pubs that young people frequented where I met and hung out with Danish guys with a mutual interest in women, hashish and elephants,---beer that is. The famous Tuburg elephant beer; they'd hit you like a stampede at night and in the morning your mouth felt like they came back and walked through it bare-foot. I just kept going back for more!

These were the descendants of the Vikings. It was apparent in their rough, but warm camaraderie, openness to new experiences and their wild sense of humor. By merely changing their clothes, they could blend right back into 'Gamle By,' the oldest part of the city, a museum really, where ancient homes from around Denmark were gathered to show how the Vikings' lived.

Check this out: I'm drinking in a pub with a bunch of Danes, mostly guys; the girls are kind of off to themselves. If a guy wants one he goes over and starts talking to her and away they go. The guys are at the bar. We're all talking and carrying on. One guy is a Danish soldier. He's got his uniform on and I see his hair hangs down past his ears. Now we're all pretty messed up, and he tells me the army issues him a hairnet to go into battle. I crack up and start laughing a little too long and too loud. He's getting a little pissed off.

He says "You know how long they teach us to fight in the army?"

I shrug my shoulders and lift my hands to say--- how long?

"Twenty-four hours"

"Really" I said. "Why's that?'

"Because by then, the Americans will be here!"

That did it. I don't know if it was the elephants, the draft or the thought of my friends dying in Vietnam, but I reached out and grabbed him by the throat, pulled him close and said "You son of a b___." That's when a few of his buddy's grab me, pin my arms back behind me and said "Easy man, easy—relax we're not at war here."

Everybody starts laughing, the soldier too. I relax as well and start laughing. But I couldn't help thinking 'shit, we're the world's policeman. I don't know how we got ourselves in this position, but I sure wish we'd get out!'

53. Two is Better than One

Liese and Anja introduced me to the best of Copenhagen from their point of view; which were mine and most any other young person at the time. I met their friends and a lot of interesting people through them both.

Get this: We had our coffee and pastries and a nice walk through town. The sun's getting lower in the sky and they say they need to go home for dinner. Liese takes my arm with her hand and squeezes gently and says "George, since you have no place to stay will you come and stay with me?"

I look deep into her eyes and tell her the truth. "I'd love to."

She smiles and says "I live with my mother and her boyfriend. It would be better if you came after eleven o'clock and knock softly."

"I'll be there." Who wouldn't I thought, even though visions of Biergedas' place in Hamburg fill my mind. What's a fellow to do?

You guessed it! Come eleven fifteen I'm scratching at her door. She lets me in, holds a finger to her lips to say shhhh and we tip-toe to her room.

What a lovely night together. Between our times of sensual bliss, we share stories of our pasts and dreams for the future. A beautiful night; all my wants, needs and desires fulfilled with a beautiful girl; wrapped tightly together, I fall into a deep sleep with not a care in the world.

Morning comes, the sun is shining through the window and I wake up to the sound of pots and pans shuffling around in the kitchen.

Oh shit! Oh God! I'm dead meat. My life starts passing before my eyes. I jump up and look out the window. It's a second story drop. I could make it if it wasn't for the bicycles parked below.

Liese wakes up and is looking a little groggy. I start waving my arms, whispering and pointing at the door but she's not getting it, nor does she seem to be too concerned.

There's a knock at the door. I take one more look at the window---know that isn't going to work, and dive back under the sheets with Liese. Might as well die here with her, besides, I don't have any clothes on.

Her mother opens the door with a tray in her hands. She sets it by the bed—looks me in the eye, smiles and says to Liese "This is for you and your friend" turns and walks out. I'm stunned! There's bread, butter, cheese, jam and coffee on the tray. I love Denmark!

We had breakfast in bed, and then went out to meet mom and the boyfriend. They were very nice. She had the same red hair as Liese and just as pretty. Her friend had the blue eyes and blonde hair but his lack of English kept him out of the conversation.

I told them I was a student and had taken a semester off from school to travel though Europe and I'd have to be back in the States pretty soon to get back to school. They liked that. She said something to Liese about a 'class' that I didn't get---till later. They both had to go to work, so Liese and I stayed there until Anja came over.

When Anja arrived we all left Liese's place together, but Liese had to go somewhere for awhile so Anja and I went to see more of the city.

It was another beautiful day as we made our way toward the old harbor known as Nyhavn. A rock break wall protected the boats form the harshness of the Sea. On an outcropping sits the "Lille Hafrue" or little mermaid. She's a bronze statue of a beautiful mermaid with long hair and a short little nose.

Anja said "She watches all the boats coming in and going out of the harbor. Every sailor retuning from a long voyage wishes she would come to life and greet them with a kiss."

I said 'I would too---she's a beautiful Dane.

We walked around the harbor and looked at the boats. Anja told me about her older sisters' friends who have a sailboat. How they sailed to the Canary Islands and back. I told her I had been there and that one day I would have a boat to travel----and I did for years.

We walked back around the harbor and stopped again at the mermaid

"She looks a little like you, Anja"

She took my hand in hers. I could feel the vibes building up to this. Her beauty radiated from inside to out and no matter which way we walked I knew we were heading to this point. I strongly desired her but knew Id' hurt Liese so I dropped her hand and said "We shouldn't do this." Boy--that came out weak. My inner conscience had trouble recognizing that.

We started heading back to meet Liese. Crossing a bridge over a canal we stopped to look at the water below.

She took my hand again, looked up at me and said "Liese and I both like you George. We've talked about this and decided to share you."

My jaw must have dropped to the railing. But I recovered quickly and asked her to reaffirm what I thought she just said. She did. Damn!! I agreed whole-heartedly--- this was an excellent idea.

By the time we got back to Liese's place she was back from her errands. We sat and talked for awhile. They said they were taking a 'sex class' in school. And then it clicked what her mother said earlier that morning about some 'class'.

"I'm ready to learn" I said. "Let the class begin."
Her mother was at work, we had the place to ourselves--- what an opportune time.

It was 'Carpe Diem'—seize the day. We did just that. Seize the day—the hour—and the moment and made the very best of them all.

We communed in each other's love and lusts until her mother was due home. During a lull in the heat and excitement, Liese told us her mother had done this when she was young with her friend and a young man. She said they pretended like they were in the old Viking days. The young man was a mighty warrior and the girls were 'ladies in waiting' and when the warrior came home from battle, they would satisfy his every need.

Nice game! It occurred to me how some would view our time together as 'dirty or sinful' while others could see the beauty in it. Right then and there I vowed to try to see the beauty that life had to show and offer---and to drink it all in excessively. That the judgments I would make would be done by weighing all the considerations and not accepting blindly those made by others with their own agenda.

~~~~

   I stayed with Liese two more days and saw as much of Copenhagen as I could, especially the free things. My money was running out and I would have to as well.
   I lived on Danish pastries, elephant beers and smørbrod. They were slices of bread or a large cracker made like an open face sandwich with ham, cheese, lieberwurst, fish or any of the other Danish delicacies. A shot of mayonnaise or mustard with a few little caviar eggs on top made them not only a work of art but a delectable delicious treat. There were whole shops dedicated to making and selling smorbrod. I believe it's the origin of our word smorgasbord; a buffet of sorts with all the different smorbrod to pick from.
   I told Liese I would leave in the morning. Anja came over early and we all said our goodbye's together. It was a sad moment, but we all new it was going to come to an end.
   Heading for the highway with my bag over my shoulder, I looked back to see them waving goodbye. It was hard leaving, I loved Denmark---but I knew I'd be back.

54. The Ferry

I made it to the ferry in good time. As I walked up to the little booth to buy a ticket, a story a guy told me in a pub came to mind. He said he rarely paid a ticket for the ferry. I thought I'd give it a try.

Two Danish officials were collecting the tickets for the ferry. After all, I was leaving Denmark for Germany.

I said "I have no money for the ticket to Germany."

They laughed and said "Then you can't get on the ferry."

"Looks like a German boat." To which they nodded their heads.

I said "I can stay here in Denmark and pan-handle the Danish people until I get the money for the ticket---or, you can let me go aboard and I'll be the German's problem." That was the 'key'. There is no love lost for the Germans. Only twenty-five years earlier they brutally occupied Denmark during World War II.

They spoke to each other for a moment, angrily turned to me and said "Get aboard and don't come back."

I passed through customs and got a free ride to Germany. But the Danes must have said something to the Germans, because when I passed through customs they did a thorough search of all my stuff. When they checked my passport and saw all the stamps and the X'ed--out Turkish stamp, they knew I wasn't their average 'six countries in six weeks' Eur-rail pass American.

I had little money and no return ticket to the States. I'd sold it at a low point in my travels, which seemed ages ago.

They thought I would become a 'burden on the state' and were leery of letting me in. I told them I had money in an account in Hamburg and gave them the name of a well known bank. They bought it.

The rides into Hamburg were pretty uneventful. I think I was feeling a little remorse---very little, for beating the Germans out of the cost of the ferry tickets. I'd had a lot of good times in Germany, but beating the system was a challenge as well as a necessity.

I never bought a ticket for the city trains or street-cars either. You bought your ticket from a vending machine or the kiosk but there were no conductors checking tickets on the trains. There were, however, transit police that would board the trains and check. If you were caught without a ticket, you got a twenty mark fine—about six fifty U.S.

For a German to be caught was a humiliation not to be born. Me—I took my chances. The cost of a ticket was about the same price as a beer in a bar. I weighed this carefully and guess which one won out?

The gig worked like this: There were usually three doors per rail car. You get in and sit near the middle. The police get on the car at each end and work toward the middle. There's always a lot of tension when they enter. Kind of like a covey of quail right before they get up and fly from danger.

The police are eye-balling everyone, if anybody makes a move for the door---they're busted. You wait calmly until the train comes to the next stop, even checking a pocket or two for that non-existing ticket. Hopefully they haven't made it to your seat yet. When the doors open don't bolt yet. If you do, one of them will jump off with you and you'll be caught.

The doors open with compressed air. When they close there's the sound of the compressed air being released,---- like a huge beer can being opened. That sound indicates you've got two seconds to get through the door. That's when you make your move, slipping out just as the doors close behind you; works most all the time.

55. The Calvary Arrives---No, It's the Navy

My last ride was from a middle aged business man in a big Mercedes sedan. What a 'boat,' like riding on air. He dropped me off in a suburb of Hamburg with an awfully familiar name—WEDEL. Heck, I've got to have some relatives here I thought. When I got to the U-bahn, or subway station, I opened a telephone book and checked out if there were any Wedel's here. There were a page and a half. It was a bit overwhelming. I shut the book—figured I'd work this out later and got on the train to the university.

I was pondering why there was so many Wedels in Wedel as the train came around 'Landensbrucken' overlooking the port. As I looked out over the port I got a terrible shock. Tied up to the pier was a huge—no—humungous American battleship with hundreds of sailors walking about. This was bad—very bad. I'd seen this before. Thousands of US sailors with pockets full of money looking for a good time. The prices of everything would go up. It happened in Barcelona. And here I was, short of money.

I got off the train at Landensbrucken and walked down to the ship to check it out. Talked with a few sailors, said I was American, and they invited me on board the ship. They gave me the tour and as we came to the mess hall, there was a bunch of guys in line for 'chow.' I asked "Hey, do ya think I could get in that line?"

"Sure man, help yourself." They said.

Did I ever 'chow down,' and mighty tasty too. You miss a few meals and you become a lot less picky as to what you'll eat. This was great!

"Hey, when's the next meal? I'll be back."

They laughed and said "Morning, noon and night."

But some of the guys gave me some pretty hard looks. Maybe because I looked like some of the anti-war demonstrators they'd seen on TV. If only they knew.

I walked up to the Reeperbahn after dinner; the 'seedier' part of the city near the port; where you could buy anything—legal or—illegal. Drugs, prostitutes sitting behind widows you could pick out like a sweet-cake, strip joints, night clubs—you name it, it was here.

Get this: Two sailors walk up to me and ask "Hey man, do you know where we can get some hash?" Ding-Ding-Ding, all the bells and whistles go off in my mind. This is it! I'm envisioning my plane ticket back to the States.

"Sure man, I can help you out."

Of course they weren't going to give me any money 'up front.' So I go to some Persians I know who sell hash, but I haven't got enough money and they won't give me any hash 'up front either. I pull out my passport and say "I'll leave this for collateral." He looks at me and his eyes narrow. He gives me the hash. He knows how valuable an American passport is.

I get right in his face, push my finger hard into his chest where his heart is and say

"Make no mistake—you'd better be here when I get back!" He smiles showing two gold capped teeth. He's there alright, when I get back. I do that a few more times until I have enough capital to keep my passport and work on my own.

I sold hash from the Persians and Germans to the sailors all night. Ate lunch and dinner aboard the ship the next day and sold hash in between and all through the night. As for sailors, there was no end to their appetite or number. This was a battle group. The aircraft carrier at the mouth of the harbor had at least five thousand guys on it. And they always have at least five destroyers and as many subs, but submarines I never saw.

While eating dinner aboard ship with a few guys, one of them tells me about the movies and lectures the navy shows them before going into port. How dangerous the locals are and the police are just as bad. I agreed.
"It's dangerous out there boys, but if you want to catch a 'buzz' while you're here, I'd be happy to help you out, being American and all---of course!"

After two long days of dealing with the sailors, I had a full belly and a wad of Yankee dollars that would choke a horse. Next stop—the airlines office. I bought a one-way cash ticket from Brussels, Belgium to New York and on to St.Louis, Missouri that was leaving in three days.

56. Homesick

I parted company with my friends in Hamburg and headed out on the road to Brussels. Two days should leave me plenty of time to get there. The rides through Germany came fast and easy as usual. Once I crossed into Belgium the momentum stopped. Rides of short distances with long waits in between became the norm. It took all day to get seventy miles. Like I wasn't meant to leave Europe, but I knew better. Too many things had fallen right into place for me to be right here—right now.

My last ride of the day: Just as a car pulls over to give me a ride, it starts raining. I jumped in and the guy asks me where I'm going.

"Brussels" I say. He's in his mid thirties, short hair and wearing a sport coat and tie.

"I can take you there."

I'm elated. It's nine o'clock and I know this is my last ride. It's never good to hitch-hike at night, I'm lucky to get this ride.

His English isn't very good, but that's alright. My Flemish is non-existent. He looks over and we smile back and forth. Hell, I'm happy. I'm out of the rain in a car going all the way to Brussels and I'm on my way home. What could be better?

He asks "Are you homesick?" Or at least that's what I think he asks. Like I said, his English isn't too good. Who cares?

"Yeah, sure" I say, turning my head, looking out the window and entering a dream world. What else could I say? Yeah I'm going home---why? I don't know; maybe to get hassled by the pigs, to get arrested for having an empty beer can in the car and slapped around for not showing the proper 'due respect' to an officer of the law. And I'm sure going to miss not to being able to buy a drink anywhere.

That's when I feel his hand on my leg. He's got my attention. I look over at him with a hard look. He smiles. I don't. Then it clicks. He didn't ask if I was homesick, he asked if I was homosexual. And I said yes! Shit!---I knock his hand off my leg and shake my index finger back and forth and say "No, No, No,"

He says he'll take me all the way to Brussels if I let him 'play' with me. Damn!
It's either that or get out. It's after nine, raining, and I know I won't get another ride tonight. Oh well.

"No"

He pulls over and I get out. We're on a two lane road, a nice residential area. I walk for a while until I come to a beautiful two story mansion surrounded by a manicured lawn and big spruce trees with their limbs hanging down to the ground. It's dry, dark and out of sight under those trees. So I unroll my sleeping bag, crawl under the huge limbs and hit the sack.

Woke up to a beautiful cloudless morning and looked at the house. A masterpiece of architecture in the light of day, especially the arched moulding over the front door and hey, what's that? Low and behold the milk man has been here. How nice! There are a couple of liters of milk and yogurt and what looks like chocolate pudding. I rolled up my sleeping bag, picked up a liter of yogurt and headed back out on the road. Hmmm, must be a lesson here. Maybe "it pays not to compromise one's principals."

I didn't have far to go. The airport is on the North side of the city and the plane wasn't leaving until four. I made it with three hours to spare. I was laughing!

57. Heading Home

The flight from Brussels to New York was pretty uneventful. The Boeing 727 was a lot smoother and faster ride than the old propeller plane I came over on six months ago. Six hours is better than thirteen. Course, there weren't any beautiful Icelandic girls pushing carts of free booze up and down the aisle either.

The flight from New York to St. Louis was full. My seat was near the middle over the wing. I stowed my stuff in the upper luggage locker and kept standing and stretching for as long as I could before having to sit down for another long flight. Not much leg room on a plane. But I wasn't complaining. The thought of being home and seeing my mom and brothers again was giving me an adrenaline rush. This has been the longest period of time I've ever been away from home.

Just before taking my seat, I look down the aisle to the back of the plane and there's my Uncle John and Aunt Ellen getting ready to sit down. Too cool. Was I glad to see them! He's one of my favorite uncles.

"Hey Uncle John—hello Aunt Ellen," I call out as I make my way toward them. I'm wearing a big smile and ready to give them a warm greeting. Uncle John's got a mean look on his face.

"Are you guys coming back from Europe too?"

"No, New York" he says, still with the mean look. I see his eyes moving as he's looking me over. The look's not changing.

"What's the matter with you boy!! You look terrible." He says. And he's probably quite right. He slept in a four star hotel last night. I slept under a tree in the rain. My hair is down to my shoulders and dirty. I'm wearing an old dirty leather sport coat I bought at the flea market in Amsterdam over a Moroccan shirt which has embroidery all over it and my jeans could probably stand up on their own. I hadn't given it much thought up till now.

"You'd better straighten up and get in line!"

I ease up to within a foot of his face and say "Don't you see---I don't want to be in that line!!!"

The disgusted look on his face said it all. I turned around, made it back to my seat and never looked back. He was one of my favorite uncles.

"Welcome home---Boy!" WOW---I changed a lot in the last six months; how naive to think the world was changing with me!

I grabbed my gear, left the plane and went down to the luggage carrousel where the action was. This would be the best place to get a ride. People were picking other people up. Everybody was happy to be home and the parking lot was just through the doors. I started asking people if they were heading in the direction of Webster Groves or Kirkwood. Finally found a middle-aged couple willing to take me. They dropped me off within a mile of my house.

I could have walked the rest of the way easy enough, but stuck my thumb out just the same. This guy almost hits me, stops, backs up, opens the door and says "Jump in. I almost ran over you, the least I can do is give you a ride." We laugh as I jump in. It's a short ride but a ride none the less.

I figure to walk the rest of the way as a car drives by, slows down to take a long look and keeps on going. "What's with that?" I wonder.

It's up the driveway and through the back door which is never locked. I can hear my bird dog 'Babe' barking a greeting from her pen behind the garage. There's my mother and my oldest brother Carl standing in the kitchen. They aren't as surprised as I would've thought as the rounds of hugs and kisses begin. What a warm wonderful greeting. My mom is so happy tears are rolling down both cheeks. She turns to my brother and says "You were right Carl, it was George walking home."
I look at Carl and slap him up-side his head 'lovingly'--- 'lovingly' is right. That's the only time I'll be able to do that without being 'tied' in a knot.

"Why didn't you pick me up?
He just laughed.

I sat down at the kitchen table with my brother. Mom opens the fridge and gets out a well worked over ham, salami and some cheese. Then gives me a beer and sits down.
This is a 'first.'

With a carving knife I cut off pieces of ham and cheese. Using the knife, I stab them one at a time and put them into my mouth as the stories begin. Mom's watching me eat with a wry smile on her face. I can't tell if it's wonder, amazement or probably just plain thankfulness that I'm home.

During a lull in the conversation, I lean back on my chair and reflect a moment on what I've just been through in the last six months. I left home with six hundred dollars, traveled through Europe for six months and came back with six hundred and fifty. As some of my experiences flashed through my mind---I couldn't help but think I made it because of the 'grace of God' and not my 'superior intellect'.

My vision and understanding of the world had expanded exponentially. The Midwest boy from St Louis had grown up. Now---I was a citizen of the world!

George Wedel
01/04/10

www.ingramcontent.com/pod-product-compliance
Lightning Source LLC
Chambersburg PA
CBHW061430040426
42450CB00007B/986